PRAISE FOR N]

In the real world, which is the world that God made, the Holy Sacrifice of the Mass is the power station feeding the life of grace. Without such grace, we die. In this volume of true stories, Fr Armand de Malleray shows us the life-giving power of the Mass in a world darkened with devildom. The light-hearted and humorous tone of the stories makes them easily readable without ignoring the gravity of the topic.

—**JOSEPH PEARCE**, author of biographies of J. R. R. Tolkien, Oscar Wilde, C. S. Lewis, and G. K. Chesterton

The unusual theme that unites a good number of the stories in this compendium is a scenario with which many a freshly-ordained priest will soon become familiar—the battle royal that often ensues in the attempt to secure an altar at which the Holy Sacrifice of the Mass may be offered in an atmosphere of recollection and decorum. With tact and good humour, Father de Malleray explores the intra-ecclesial prejudices and neuroses which have given rise to such a state of affairs, and illustrates how perseverance, charity and prayer are the most effective weapons we possess against suspicion and bigotry. An edifying read for both priests and laity, which we should pray will contribute to the healing of self-inflicted wounds which for too long have hampered the Church's mission of evangelisation.

—**FR JULIAN LARGE**, Provost of the London Oratory

The stories in this collection give us precious evidence of the hidden persistence of the grace of the true priestly vocation in unexpected situations. The ten narratives portray priestly candidates and priests of various ages and cultures. All reveal that secret dialogue in the soul that takes place when grace is at work. Based on my experience in teaching Thomistic philosophy to seminarians for a decade and catechesis to seminarians and priests as well as lay people, I cannot recommend this book highly enough for young Catholic men and for all those who nurture vocations, or who could, but who are not sufficiently alert to the quiet presence of the Holy Spirit in many young souls.

— **DR CAROLINE FAREY**, *Annunciation Catechesis*

In *Near Missed Masses*, Fr de Malleray finds a delightfully playful and imaginative way to reinvent true contemporary stories and drive home a serious point: the value of the Holy Sacrifice of the Mass, and the zeal that we should have to celebrate (as priests) or attend (as layfaithful) this Sacrifice worthily and frequently. In this way, the book functions like the proverbial storeroom containing things both new and old!

— **FR HENRY WHISENANT**, Diocese of East Anglia (UK)

Near Missed Masses

NEAR Missed Masses

TEN SHORT STORIES
BASED ON ACTUAL EVENTS

Fr Armand de Malleray, FSSP

AROUCA
PRESS

Publication authorised on 4th September 2020 by
Very Rev Fr Andrzej Komorowski, Superior General FSSP.

The author thanks the various priests and laity
who generously gave time to proof-read the
book and suggest valuable modifications.

Copyright © Arouca Press 2021
Copyright © Armand de Malleray, FSSP

All rights reserved:
No part of this book may be reproduced or transmitted,
in any form or by any means, without permission

ISBN: 978-1-989905-48-7 (pbk)
ISBN: 978-1-989905-49-4 (hc)

Arouca Press
PO Box 55003
Bridgeport PO
Waterloo, ON N2J3G0
Canada
www.aroucapress.com
Send inquiries to info@aroucapress.com

CONTENTS

INTRODUCTION

MEA CULPA! A CONFESSION IS NEEDED FIRST, gentle reader. Here it is: I once denied a fellow priest access to an altar for his Holy Mass. I had excuses, having just been assigned to a church in a distant diocese, when some unknown voice over the phone requested to say Mass in an Eastern rite that same Sunday afternoon, for an ethnic group locked out of their habitual place of worship. Taken by surprise, and unsure whether the request was genuine, or what uncustomary liturgical requirements that Eastern rite Mass might involve, I referred the caller to the local pastor who had authority to provide for him. I added that, should the pastor not be reached in time, the stranded priest could of course call me back. I never heard from him again. But my coffee cup tasted slightly bitter, later that afternoon, despite having looked forward to it as a reward after a terribly busy Sunday morning. I couldn't help imagining this fellow priest, possibly in dire straits, wandering with his pilgrim flock in the cold December rain. That Advent, had I turned away the Eucharistic Lord like the selfish innkeeper did Our Lady with Child and St Joseph in Bethlehem? *"Knock, knock, knock, we need a place to stay."* Admittedly, the innkeeper of old hadn't *seen* the divine Child, although He was soon to appear. Similarly, I hadn't quite turned Christ away, God forbid, only his priest: but by so doing, had I not prevented the Lord from appearing on the altar of sacrifice? Knock, knock, knock, at one's priestly conscience ... And are not all the Holy Masses to be offered until Judgment Day numbered in God's Providence? Who then would dare to prevent even one from taking place, lest he or she were asked to account for the graces lost?

Looking back, I wish I had been more welcoming to that alleged priest over the phone. Admittedly, I had lacked time and knowledge of the local situation to offer the best response.

In fairness then, this book will only consider occasions when priests and laity had ample time to understand the petition and every means to grant it safely, or at least were free not to interfere. None of them can have ignored what I also had been taught, namely: that nothing matters more than the Holy Sacrifice of the Mass, the unbloody re-enactment of Christ's redeeming Sacrifice on Calvary. Or didn't they know what I had learnt? — that every Catholic priest in good standing has a strict right to offer Holy Mass in any Catholic church at any suitable time. Unlike me perhaps, they hadn't experienced helplessness and frustration when being unjustly prevented from offering Mass. This occurred when travelling, or on holiday, or on pilgrimage. Numerous times in various countries, despite having informed in advance the parish I would visit; despite producing a freshly stamped *celebret*; despite displaying a friendly smile and declaring myself ready to accept the least inconvenient time and location available (such as an auxiliary chapel or a crypt); despite giving assurances that I had every relevant liturgical item with me — I was turned away. On the contrary, let me now thank from my heart the many, many priests, sacristans and sisters who did, more or less readily, welcome me.

Now in my twentieth year as a priest, I wished to put in writing some of those experiences, whether my own or those encountered by fellow priests. Why? First, to encourage priests to persevere in offering Holy Mass daily. Second, to draw the Catholic laity's attention to this unsuspected battle which observant clergy often must fight in sacristies, airport chapels, shrines, etc. Of set purpose I shall not consider the spectacularly more numerous and tragic cases of priests persecuted in their ministry by *enemies* of the Church. I have narrated elsewhere the heart-breaking story of Bl. Karl Leisner, for instance, a German seminarian imprisoned by the Nazis and ordained a priest in secret in Dachau, only to die after having offered Holy Mass a single time. Neither will I include natural catastrophes, such as the 2016 earthquake in Norcia, Italy, which compromised Holy Mass in the Benedictine crypt until the courageous celebrant risked his life to retrieve the Blessed Sacrament. How many more similar stories could be told? Before these my martyred or heroic fellow priests, I bow with reverence and gratitude for such supernatural witness, and I smile at the comparatively mild trials which I and many other priests suffered for the celebration of Holy Mass at the hands of sacristans, priests and sometimes bishops. We were not tortured. We were not killed. We were only inconvenienced.

To be precise, then, the specific purpose of this book is to illustrate opposition from *within* Holy Church, not from without. These ten short stories describe hindrances to the celebration of Holy Mass inflicted on innocent priests by Catholics in good standing and, strangely, meaning well. They didn't oppose the celebration of Holy Mass for political or religious motives, as in other contexts Mohammedans, Buddhists, Hindus, Protestants, Vikings, Huns, Iroquois, Marxists, secularists and others did, or still do. No, these Catholics prevented it, or tried to, because they failed to recognise that, given a suitable time frame and with permission requested in Christian courtesy, Holy Mass offered in conformity with the rubrics takes precedence over any other activity and any other consideration. The obstacles put between priests and altars are of various kinds. They can be caused by flawed theology, family jealousy, social considerations, clerical ambition, liturgical innovation, cowardice, sheer sloth, viral diseases, or something else yet. In most cases, several such factors combine. One must pause here and look the beast in the eye if I may say, that is, one must confront the utter gravity of unjust hindrances put up against the celebration of Holy Mass by those whose chief mission is to facilitate it, by virtue of their ordination or baptism. We mustn't coddle that beast; we mustn't call it our pet. (I insert a disclaimer here in advance; the reader should know that the ten stories involve despotic cats and lazy dogs, a stuffed bear and fast horses, plus real-life noisy birds!) Back to our topic, this rampant Eucharistic abuse is deeply wrong; and the tragedy is that we have become so used to it that we do not realise its malice anymore. The abuse is threefold. The offense is first and foremost against God, whose extrinsic glory increases each time the Holy Sacrifice of the Mass is offered. Secondly, the harm is inflicted on souls, which are deprived of the temporal application of Christ's saving merits that Holy Mass effectuates. Finally, violence is exerted against the priest whose ontological *raison d'être* is to offer the divine Victim. On Judgment Day, an account will be asked of us Catholics for each and every such Eucharistic abuse.

In mid-Lent 2020 the public celebration of Holy Mass was suspended all over the world. One year later, the crisis is far from being over. This unprecedented calamity had at least the advantage of manifesting three important truths about the Holy Eucharist as a sacrifice and as a sacrament. First, bishops publicly asked their priests to continue offering Holy Mass daily: even alone, even behind locked doors, even without live streaming. Although such injunctions might not surprise Catholics with a traditional formation, they contrast spectacularly with the customs in force across most of the ecclesiastical spectrum. Up to the Covid-19 lockdown, offering Holy Mass seemed justified in proportion with the number of persons physically present in the pews. In consequence, many priests routinely dispensed with it on their day off, on holiday or when travelling. Second, priests learnt to offer Holy Mass even without fellow priests standing at the altar. Up to then, sacramental concelebration was expected whenever several priests were present in a church. This had led many priests seldom to celebrate individually. In that context, the permission granted by the Holy See indirectly reaffirmed the lawfulness of the mono-celebration of the Holy Sacrifice of the Mass: "*in the countries which have been struck by the disease and where restrictions around the assembly and movement of people have been imposed, Bishops and priests may celebrate the rites of Holy Week without the presence of the people and in a suitable place, avoiding concelebration"* (Robert Cardinal Sarah, Congregation for Divine Worship and the Discipline of the Sacraments, Decree on 25 March 2020). A third re-discovery for many was the insistence on spiritual Communion. Despite the loss of sacramental Holy Communion, what joy for Catholics with a traditional formation to see numerous bishops and priests starting to promote what the Council of Trent had already taught (following St Thomas Aquinas), praising, *"those who, eating in desire that heavenly bread which is set before them, are, by a lively faith which worketh by charity, made sensible of the fruit and usefulness thereof"* (Session 13, Chapter 8).

If these three Eucharistic truths were universally acknowledged and implemented even after normal liturgical life resumes, a little book like the present one would soon be outdated. I wish it may be the case. It would also lessen or eliminate the bias that persists in some quarters against our shared patrimony as Roman Catholics, namely, the Extraordinary Form liturgy. Several priest characters in this book sometimes attend or offer the New Mass in the vernacular. I didn't wish to suggest that the opposition was merely down to New Mass against traditional Mass. Undoubtedly, many priests do go to great lengths to offer their daily Mass in the New rite even when away from home. However, it is a fact that the more a priest offers the traditional Mass, the less he will accept to spend one day without offering Holy Mass—singly and reverently at that. Outside their parishes, such priests are therefore more likely to meet some opposition. Their insistence or perseverance can be perceived as somehow associated with the traditional liturgy. In contrast, priests who readily concelebrate or skip daily Mass will be spared confrontation with the host priest or his sacristan — something no priest seeks, especially if travelling or on holiday.

Sadly, even after such Eucharistic sufferings imposed world-wide for the sake of virus containment, wilful ignorance still hinders the legitimate celebration of Holy Mass, as I experienced yet again. The following anecdote is given by way of illustration. Last summer (2020) I emailed the priest in charge of a national shrine in some part of the world for permission to take a group of pilgrims and offer Holy Mass at the tombs of the saints displayed in that church (little visited, paradoxically). His response seemed to have been written thirty-seven years ago, at the time of *Quatuor Abhinc Annos* (1984), the earlier relaxation of the restrictions towards the traditional Roman liturgy. It informed me that *"there are in the Diocese of N. designated churches where officially the Extraordinary Form takes place. St X. is not one of those churches. You are most welcome to visit the Shrine but this parish has no permission to celebrate Mass in the Extraordinary Form."* That in 2020 a parish pastor and rector of a national shrine might be ignorant of the motu proprio *Ecclesia Dei* (1988) and even more so of *Summorum Pontificum* (2007) is disturbing. But once reassured that every priest in the Latin Church has permission to offer or host Holy Mass in that form, if the same rector persists in denying an altar to chaplain and pilgrims, the situation is serious. This latest incident confirmed to me that, sadly, my ten little stories are not yet history. This ongoing problem deserves documenting for the common good of the Church.

However, the stories needed to be written in a positive light. The putrid smell of vindictiveness should be avoided at any cost, as opposed to the reconciliatory and constructive goal of the book. Humour should be used then, as a reminder to take oneself and one's afflictions light-heartedly under God's benign Providence. *Christian* humour is meant here, not bitter irony and destructive sarcasm. Deference has been shown to all

alluded to in the book, particularly those endowed with ecclesiastical dignity such as bishops and priests. With the same aim
for amicable levity, dogmatic argumentation has been left out
to keep each narrative moving swiftly. (The inquisitive reader is
welcome to consult the list of books at the end of this volume,
including doctrinal titles on the Most Holy Eucharist and the
Sacred Priesthood by the same author.) To foster entertainment,
the original stories were selected and told in connection with
diverse continents and cultures. This reflects how widespread is
the Catholic opposition faced by would-be celebrants of Holy
Mass in many parts of the world. Combining these parameters
was challenging at times, as certain truths cannot be described,
however neutrally, without causing righteous indignation. Con-
sequently, many of the conflicts depicted in the ten stories were
actually attenuated. If any twist in what the innocent characters undergo strikes the reader as unjust, let him assume
that the original situation was worse. Understandably, nearly
all names of persons and places were altered. Nothing in the
stories allows identification of the original protagonists, so that
any alleged resemblance with existing persons or past events
would be fortuitous and irrelevant. But most facts, especially
some salient features in each story, actually happened. They
are real-life events, even though independent circumstances
were sometimes combined and threads interwoven to enrich
the plot. Dear reader, this little book is not about one priest or
several; it is not even about rights and wrongs. It is about the
Holy Sacrifice of the Mass, the main vehicle of our redemption,
and its more frequent, welcome, and fruitful celebration. May
Our Blessed Lady foster this outcome for us, to the greater
glory of God and of their Son Jesus, our Saviour.

Warrington, England
22nd February 2021

I

Chum of the Lord

(1994, FRANCE)

"RUTHLESS, THEY SAY HE IS! BUT I WAS warned to cut my hair pretty short in anticipation so that, with some luck, this Sergeant Boucher might spare my scalp. Especially as our platoon was to enter the saloon at 4pm. Boucher is now twenty minutes behind schedule. Having already shaved dozens of heads, he will be glad to turn away those in no dire need of his skills."

Private Yannick Kergrist thanked his fellow soldier for the tip offered (albeit too late), while combing his hair with his fingers. Surely not short enough for Boucher... Interiorly though, Yannick did not mind the thorough military head shaving inflicted on the raw recruits. As he watched the fair curls of the young man before him fall to the ground under the relentless blade of Sergeant Boucher, Yannick spontaneously recalled the sheep shearing of his childhood, back at the farm. There was something altogether brutal and tender in the way the animals were relieved of their wool.

He couldn't have been older than twelve when for the first time he had led the flock back from the Kentonnaz pastures: a three-mile walk across the well-known countryside of his native Brittany. It occurred on a hot summer afternoon after a heavy rain. In Yannick's memory, the very peculiar smell of humid and hot tarmac always conjured up the heavy odour of the sheep. Another six years had gone by and...

"Next!"

Sergeant Boucher was not to be kept waiting. Now a young recruit perched on the barber's stool in the army base outside Nîmes in Provence, Yannick wondered how long God would need to turn him from sheep to shepherd... of souls. His mind was set on entering seminary at the end of his military service. Clerics of old would have their hair cut, Yannick had read. Could this free tonsure administered by Sergeant Boucher on behalf of the French Republic count as a first step towards the clerical state and the altar of God?

*   *   *

Later that week, queuing outside the armoury to receive his automatic rifle, Yannick caught a reflection of his face in the window. It had been three days since his arrival at the Nîmes army barracks and his shaven skull still looked like a monk's, no doubt. Behind him, two fellow-soldiers were bitterly complaining about the news broken the day before: all recruits were grounded on their first weekend — girlfriends would have to wait until the following week. This was inhumane! What did the brass think the troops were made of? Yannick was concerned as well, for a different reason though. Would he be able to attend Holy Mass this Sunday, he wondered? Would he receive Christ in Holy Communion? When would the captain tell him whether or not his request had been granted?

On hearing that there would be no getting out of the camp, he had respectfully raised the question of Sunday worship. The appointed padre was away on operations somewhere in Africa. How would Yannick and any other Catholic privates be able to fulfil their religious obligation? Surely, an exception could be made for them to worship in town that Sunday. Corporal Mardeau had looked at the young man with surprise before sending him to the lieutenant. The lieutenant was not opposed, but did not think he had the authority to grant such a request.

On his way to the captain's office, Yannick smiled interiorly at the perplexity displayed by the military hierarchy. "If this does not suffice, will they take me to the colonel?" It really sounded as if he had asked for something totally unexpected, like demanding spring rolls on the grounds of an allergy to any food other than Oriental. Was he the very first Catholic on this base? Had no young man within these walls ever stated his Catholic identity? If he had been a professional football player due for an important game, he bet the officer would have been more likely to grant him leave. The captain told Yannick that he would give his answer soon.

Half an hour later, the five platoons were standing in line in front of the trucks, each man carrying his rifle on his shoulder. This was to be their first drill outside the camp. Yannick was glad to be able to get out, even if only to crawl in the dust and sweat under the unremitting Mediterranean sun. "At ease!" Corporal Mardeau gazed across the dozens of young faces still unfamiliar to him, which head shaving had made less distinctive. He looked slightly embarrassed, in contrast with his normally assertive countenance. After a while, with some level of annoyance, he shouted: "Now *where* is he, the chum of the Lord, the Mass-goer?"

Men laughed at this rather uncommendable qualification. Yannick was pretty sure this was about his petition for Sunday Mass. But there and then, before all his comrades, he suddenly felt ashamed, as if something private to him was about to be discussed before all. After a silence, he dared utter: "Is it me you want, Sir?" Mardeau came to him and intimated briskly: "Captain Tourasse granted your request. And I will come along to that Mass."

Shouting towards the platoon, Mardeau explained: "As an exception, any Catholic here is given permission to attend Sunday Mass this weekend. It will be on Saturday evening at St Monica Church, in the city centre. You must wear civilian clothes. It is strictly forbidden to leave the group as we walk to the church and back. No one will be allowed out of the camp unless his name figures on the list. You have until the end of breakfast tomorrow to sign up. Ask Private Kergrist to put your name down. Now get into the bloody trucks, we're already late!"

While the vehicles loaded with soldiers raced towards the training moor some five miles away, young men congratulated Yannick, tossed about upon the uncomfortable benches: "Clever move you made, buddy: you'll get to walk a free man this weekend, even if only for an hour! You might even manage to twist Mardeau's arm and get a beer on the way."

Back at the barracks that evening, all rifles thoroughly cleaned up and locked up at the armoury, a surprise awaited Yannick after his much-needed shower. More and more young men were asking him to add their names to the Sunday Mass list. He recalled that mass conversions had taken place in Church history, like on the day of Pentecost in Jerusalem. Had the Holy Ghost suddenly enlightened his fellow soldiers? What fervour, suddenly! What devotion! The Nîmes Regiment was not exactly Jerusalem, but if the prospect of a free stroll across town in civvies — and of smiling girls walking by — could bring some of the proselytes one step closer to God at Holy Mass, why not give thanks for it?

On the Saturday evening, walking to the church took less than thirty minutes. Rare were the soldiers who seemed genuine believers, judging from their behaviour. Only a few knew when to kneel and where to look, namely, towards the altar and the tabernacle. Most of the others vaguely attempted a sign of the cross on entering, and remained at the rear, closely watched by Corporal Mardeau. They would not try to escape, Mardeau knew, after his warning: "Any one misbehaving will be grounded next weekend again."

Altogether, it had gone pretty well, Yannick thought at the end. He had done the first reading from the ambo. Receiving the Lord in Holy Communion renewed his confidence (he'd declined the offer to assist the priest in distributing the Sacrament). His next twelve months in the army were not a very pleasant prospect without a padre nearby, and his priestly vocation was still a remote possibility. But this near missed

Sunday Mass felt like a providential encouragement. Of course, he realised, if he ever became a priest, he would get to offer Mass whenever and wherever he wanted.

Outside the church, parishioners greeted the soldiers. The congregation was old, with barely a couple of families in attendance. Understandably, the sight of such a large group of healthy and shaven young men at Mass had caused quite a sensation. The people spoke to them with kindness, as if they had known the visitors for a long time.

After Corporal Mardeau had checked on his flock, all walked back to the base. As Yannick came towards the building of his platoon, two soldiers sitting on the floor mocked the Mass-goers asking: "So, does it taste good, the Body of Christ?" Yannick felt sorry for them and would not respond. But Tross, next to him, would not have it. Trouble was likely to occur since Tross, of African descent, was the tallest man in the platoon and was built like an Olympic basket-ball player. Instead of punching the offenders, though, he uttered in a very measured voice: "You are small." Yannick thought that it said it all, while he pitied those grown men whose spiritual stature was still so diminutive, sadly.

* * *

A few weeks later, the padre came back. Yannick met him in the old sacristy where the priest was busy throwing old books into a large bin, together with some Mass vestments and half burnt candles. A middle-sized man in his sixties, the padre was wearing civvies and smiled when Yannick saluted him: "At ease, boy. So, you're the baby soldier Mardeau told me about: 'Jesus' chum'? Good, you can help me finish clearing up this junk at last. The colonel confirmed last month that our Nîmes barracks will be decommissioned next autumn. Bad luck, yours is probably the last year in this country with compulsory military service. It was time this ended: that will all save you

time. And if Russia wanted to invade us, how long could you
hold them up anyway?"

Soon enough the bin was full, and both sat down on a bench.
Yannick told the priest about his life, also offering to serve
Mass. Surprisingly, the padre was not particularly enthusiastic
when Yannick mentioned his desire to become a priest. He
suggested instead to spend several years in the world, or indeed,
to enlist for good at the regiment. Had Yannick a girlfriend?
No? Well, rushing into seminary without knowing the love
of a woman could lead to catastrophes once ordained. Work
experience was also needed to meet people where they were.
Dismissively, he added that there had been no need to make a
fuss for Mass on the first Sunday, since military confinement
dispensed Catholics from the Sunday obligation. Yannick was
surprised by the priest's reaction.

"Excuse me Father, but if the Mass is the centre of our lives
as Catholics, should we not do everything in our power to
attend or offer it, even daily?" The padre looked at him with
sympathy, explaining: "In theory you're right, boy. But after
decades of active ministry, I have learnt that most people are
not really interested in sharing blessed bread and wine with me.
So, if they don't come to church, I must go to them instead and
share their lives as they are and... How to put it? And pull
down the barrier of clericalism—a big word. Call me Gilles,
by the way, just like I call you Yannick, not 'Private Kergrist.'
Men are more than their name tags."

Yannick made an effort, venturing: "Okay Fath... I mean,
Gilles. But once you've explained to people that the Mass is
the saving sacrifice of Christ, surely they want to come and be
saved, don't they?" Gilles smiled and grasped a book from the
bin. "Just before you walked in, I had browsed through this
old manual. You're much too young to remember what rubbish
was put in people's mind before we changed all that. I must
read this bit to you. Now, that's going to be a shock to your

system boy, but you'll thank me for it. Just listen to how they listed every gesture as if it carried magical power, and boasted of such a fuss. I had a narrow escape, having been ordained in 1970, just when the new liturgy came into force. Now we've liberated the Spirit. Listen to this..."

Sixteen times does the celebrant make the sign of the cross upon his own person; six times he turns to the people; eight times he kisses the altar; eleven times he raises his eyes to heaven; ten times he strikes his breast, and as many times he genuflects; no less than fifty-four times he joins his hands; he bows his head or his whole person thirty times; he makes the sign of the cross over the oblation thirty-one times; sometimes he prays with arms extended, more often with folded hands...

The priest glanced at Yannick, claiming with a smile: "I heard you snore! Wake up, it's not finished yet." He read further: *Nine times he lays his left hand upon the altar; eleven times he places it upon his breast; eight times he raises both hands to heaven; eleven times he prays silently; thirteen times he prays audibly; ten times the chalice is covered, and uncovered; twenty times the priest moves to and fro before the altar.*

Yannick listened to the mocking voice of the padre, wondering what to think. He felt a bit overwhelmed by the lengthy enumeration, but also by the realisation that believers of old took each ritual gesture so seriously. Gilles stopped and handed the book to Yannick, challenging him: "Your turn to read, if you dare!" The young man started with embarrassment, as he was becoming aware of a surge of awe in his heart, which he knew was better concealed, for the present:

These oft-repeated ceremonies and some hundred and fifty others are enjoined upon the priest who celebrates Mass. In addition the rubrics to be followed are four hundred in number; these the priest who says Mass according to the Roman ordo is bound strictly to observe, under pain of sin. For all this ritual has a mystic meaning, and contributes to the proper and reverent performance of this holy and sublime act. On this account Pope St Pius V strictly commanded that, in virtue of holy obedience, all cardinals, archbishops, bishops, prelates, and priests should say Mass in this and no other manner, without diverging in any way from it, either by addition or suppression. If a priest willingly and wittingly alters or omits any of these ceremonies, it is not to be reckoned as a slight carelessness on his part, but as a grievous sin, since it is not merely an offence against the honour and dignity of the highest act of worship, but a violation of the express law of the Church.

Father Gilles snatched the book from Yannick's hands and threw it back into the bin. Had he noticed or only guessed the impact of the reading upon the heart of the would-be seminarian? He laughed: "Sorry I inflicted this on you, boy. I thought it not a bad thing for you to have heard it once at least. Although the new ways are all you've ever known, the contrast should make you value them better. They brought us such freedom, such spontaneity!"

That evening in the dormitory room, while a few men lying on their beds were shamelessly looking at "adult" magazines, Yannick was the one experiencing guilt while browsing through Fr Martin Cochem's *Explanation of the Holy Sacrifice of the Mass*. It bore the fascinating mention of a "Copyright, 1896 by Benziger Brothers, Einsiedeln"—nearly a hundred years earlier. He had not been able to resist the urge to save the antiquated volume from the dumpster, after Fr Gilles had asked him to empty the sacristy bin on his way out. The vestments he hadn't dared retrieve. But he had kept an old altar missal in addition, which he was anxious to examine during his next free time. As he closed Fr Cochem's book, he noticed that the author was a Franciscan who had died as long ago as 1712. And yet, how strangely the dead priest's words resonated in the young man's heart, suggesting that Mass was something even more serious than he had thought, something arousing the passions of men, something a priest was accountable for. Could he ever meet the challenge?

By a happy coincidence, Yannick was pleased to discover later on that the barracks was built on the site of a former Franciscan friary confiscated by the State during the French Revolution. Many friars would have prayed and offered or attended Holy Mass on this spot. He asked them for guidance from heaven, as he was feeling a bit unsettled in his understanding of the Mass and of the priesthood. The holy friars would surely intercede for him, that in God's own time, hopefully, he might stand at the altar of God and offer the divine Victim in the person of Christ — as Fr Cochem put it — for the glory of God and the salvation of souls, starting with his own. Please God, he prayed, that he might never through his own fault miss an occasion of offering Holy Mass.

II

Heimatprimiz, or First Mass Home
(2000, GERMANY)

D EACON WALTER HOPED THAT HIS DEEP
sigh of relief had not been noticed, as he sat on the
edge of his chair, in the Seminary Rector's office. The
last door had opened up, it seemed, securing his priestly ordination, there in Bavaria. Father Rector had just announced to
him that the favourable vote by the Seminary Council had been
confirmed by the Superior General of the Fraternity. Thus, in
four months, by the end of June 2000, Walter would become
a priest, along with ten of his classmates. Only then did he
remember to bring out of his cassock pocket his left fist, tightly
clenched around his rosary beads since the beginning of the
meeting. Shy by temperament, Walter managed to let a gentle
smile express his gratitude, while pretending to clean his glasses.
A priest for the Third Millennium—a Catholic priest forever!
What joy, after nearly seven years of hard work! He gave thanks
to God for such a decisive step and left the Rector's office with
a little head bow, shutting the thick door behind him with quiet
application. He felt quite ready: that is, as much as a young
man can be when about to be made another Christ.

The ordination ceremony would be taken care of by the seminary staff and fellow seminarians according to their respective
competences: sacristans, schola singers, masters of ceremony,
flower arrangers and even the photocopy team putting together
the order of service. They were all used to it, having to perform
the same complex liturgies several times a year for Minor and
Major ordinations. On the other hand, back home, no one
knew how to prepare a First Solemn High Mass. That would
be the challenge, the young cleric anxiously admitted. There
was no time to lose and, immediately after having broken the

good news to his family, pulling himself together, Walter wrote to the parish priest, requesting a suitable date for the First Mass in his native Staufferburg, in the *Martinskirche*, that is, St Martin's village church.

Staufferburg was not even a small town. Situated in the rural diocese of Brausach, about an hour from Cologne, it was set in a traditionally Catholic part of Germany. Deacon Walter's family had lived there for centuries. They had rebuilt the current church after the Thirty Years War, but only in 1716 had the famous baroque façade been added, after a design by the celebrated Balthasar Neumann. Walter happily recalled studying this aspect of local history at university. However, for a dozen years now, the ancestral carved pews below the family coat of arms in the sanctuary were left empty. Before retiring, the last resident parish priest Fr Johannes had warned Walter's family: "I did all I could to keep things as I had found them, as we had always done here. But my successor has modern ideas, I am told. If you want peace with *Pfarrer* Kugel, perhaps it would be better to sit in the nave with everybody, anywhere suitable in front of the new altar. Sadly, the signal services rendered by your family to this parish might even be held against you."

The most visible change had been the drop in standards of reverence towards the Blessed Sacrament. Old Fr Johannes had been offering the modern Mass of course, in German, but with noticeable recollection and at the high altar. His zeal to organise the yearly Corpus Christi procession was a wonderful witness. On that occasion the *Staufferstrasse*, the steep high street of the village, was decorated with patterns of coloured sawdust framed with flowers, depicting chalices, crosses, pelicans and other Eucharistic symbols. As an altar boy, Walter had walked by Fr Johannes's side, carrying the burse with the corporal. The priest, his hands wrapped in the *Schultervelum*, the cloth-of-gold humeral veil, was holding the gilded monstrance with the Lord Jesus in its midst, under the velvet canopy which four men skilfully manoeuvred along the awkward curves of the medieval street. This devotion, and more, had stopped with *Pfarrer* Kugel's arrival.

To be fair, unlike Fr Johannes, *Pfarrer* Kugel did not reside at Staufferburg but at the nearby town, whence he drove every Sunday to one of the four churches now amalgamated as one new parish. He was very busy and had had to make drastic managerial decisions. Fortnightly, when no Sunday Mass was taking place at Staufferburg, Eucharistic services were available instead. They were conducted by Dr Heike Reich, a learned woman who had studied theology in Tübingen with *Pfarrer* Kugel, and for whom the full-time position of *Pastoralreferentin*, that is, "pastoral counselloress," had been created (with fitting wages). On those Sundays, Walter's parents had started attending neighbouring churches, wherever Holy Mass was offered. Walter had had few opportunities to meet *Pfarrer* Kugel, having been away at seminary for nearly seven years. His First Mass would be a providential occasion to improve the relationship with the local pastor, Walter hoped, and to give the parish a rare occasion to celebrate together.

Less than a week later, *Pfarrer* Kugel's response arrived. Its tone was professional and courteous, but its contents left the young deacon shattered. While congratulating Walter on his forthcoming ordination, *Pfarrer* Kugel stated that the schedule of liturgies and other activities planned all across the extended parish had long ago been put together and agreed with the various parish council members. At Staufferburg that Sunday, what was programmed was a Eucharistic service, not a Mass. Dr Heike Reich would welcome Walter's participation though, if he wished to give a homily or help with distributing the Bread and Wine. A stipend would be allocated according to diocesan rates for a visiting cleric. As to Walter's secondary petition, namely, to offer Mass daily at the *Martinskirche*, the same parish church, during his week spent at home before and

after the First Mass, it was granted, provided only his close
relatives attended and no publicity was made.

While rubbing his handkerchief against his wet palms, Walter could not reconcile this response with what he had been
taught at seminary about Holy Mass and the sacred priesthood.
Nothing was more important than Holy Mass, he knew well.
And every priest had a duty to foster priestly vocations to the
best of his abilities. But there had been no man ordained to the
priesthood at Staufferburg in the villagers' memory. Sure, some
young men had become lay brothers at the nearby Benedictine
abbey (of which his great-great-great-great-uncle had been the
abbot) before the Napoleonic wars led to its secularisation;
and in the late nineteenth century, several girls had joined a
nursing order of nuns, one of the few allowed by Chancellor
Bismarck's anti-Catholic *Kulturkampf*. But what of *priests*? Walter was apparently the first one in centuries. Was that not an
occasion to give thanks to God, regardless of his own many
flaws and his inexperience? How could a Eucharistic service
possibly be given precedence over the celebration of the Holy
Sacrifice of the Mass, let alone a new priest's First Mass? "And
in a church built by my own family," thought Walter, blushing
as he realised that such a circumstance gave him no particular
right over what was a public action of the Church. Were *Pfarrer* Kugel and Dr Reich unaware of the fact that a Eucharistic
service was simply not the Sacrifice of the Mass, so that its
fruits were much less than those of Holy Mass, regardless of
the participants' good intentions?

Admittedly, Walter had expected some level of opposition.
He knew that the traditional Roman liturgy was still frowned
upon by many clergy. But his priestly community had been
founded twelve years earlier by decision of Pope John-Paul II
and with direct involvement of Cardinal Joseph Ratzinger, the
current Prefect of the Congregation for the Doctrine of the
Faith. His Eminence, Bavarian by birth, had even attended

the Easter Vigil at Walter's seminary near Lake Constance and offered a solemn Easter Sunday Mass, all this in the traditional Latin rite. If that was not enough to demonstrate that Walter's community was in full communion with Rome, then what would? The date could not be changed either, as Walter was needed as chaplain for a youth camp later on in July, while most available seminarians would be away on holiday in August, leaving him without sufficient assistance to prepare and perform the complex ceremony. Looking towards the Alps through his seminary window, he felt powerless and rather overwhelmed. His First Mass back home seemed a more remote reality than the distant mountains.

* * *

Back with his family after Holy Week and Easter, Walter was discussing the issue for the umpteenth time, now with Martin, his elder brother by fourteen years and a local politician. Their father had gone for a walk with the dogs to calm down, so fed up he was with the "*Pfarrer* Kugel Circus." Walter also knew that his father was annoyed by his late attempt to book the church. Admittedly, the young cleric had found it presumptuous to ask *Pfarrer* Kugel until the seminary Rector had confirmed his promotion to the priesthood. Would he have been more successful a year in advance? As to his mother, he felt that she was sad for him, although she did not fully understand why he would not say the modern Mass in Latin on this occasion, if it made things easier with *Pfarrer* Kugel.

The mother of the future priest had kept to herself a conversation overheard that morning as she walked through the frosty graveyard, a shortcut between the *Martinskirche* and the family hall. High above, through the sacristy window left ajar despite the chill, cigarette smoke rose together with a woman's voice, now answering with some level of upset: "It would help if you stopped laughing, Father. Of course I never meant that there

were Japanese at the Crusades! I wonder who ever misquoted
me like that. Why should my doctorate in pastoral theology
make me such an *ignoramus* in basic history? All I said — let
me repeat it *verbatim* to avoid any misunderstanding — is: 'That
family has learned nothing since their time in the Crusades, or
merely since the end of the Holy Roman Empire. They remind
one of Japanese soldiers on Pacific islands, who kept fighting
years after the end of World War II, unable to believe that their
emperor had surrendered.' I don't care what the ...." Above
the head of Walter's mother, the slammed window muted the
end of the conversation. Slightly embarrassed at her unintended
eavesdropping, she had little doubt as to who that seemingly
outdated family was, as well as the two interlocutors. Fuelled
by her motherly pride, indignation rose in her heart, blossom-
ing on her lips into a vengeful smile as she realised that this
unsuspected division within the adverse party could be taken
advantage of. As her eyes met the cemetery crucifix though,
she immediately checked her thoughts and mentally affirmed:
"There is no adverse party. There are no parties at all. There is
but one Lord and all of us His children. And I won't mention
what I heard."

In the dining hall after lunch, standing by the hearth as the
weather was still chilly, the older son Martin suggested that
Walter should go to Brausach and meet with Bishop Braunmüller. The visit should not be intended as lobbying, but simply
as an opportunity to introduce himself further and ask His
Lordship's blessing on his pending ministry as a priest. "Why
not," Martin added with a smile of intelligence, "present the
Bishop with a copy of your book?" Walter considered the suggestion with a mixture of joy and unease. His book? Yes, that
could be a way of showing His Lordship that despite being a
traditional deacon, he was more open-minded than expected.
The book was a short one, based on Walter's dissertation for his
Bachelor's degree at Cologne University. Its full title was *West*

German Baroque as an inspiration for the New Evangelisation: How sacred architecture helped revive the faith during and after the Enlightenment. At his father's insistence, a simplified version of the text had been printed for relatives and friends—a mere hundred copies—with a few lines granted as foreword by an obliging cardinal from Rome. In retrospect, Walter was glad that his modest work had been made available to a wider audience than his university tutor and jury. Although the young cleric dreaded the attention of strangers, perhaps offering a copy of the book to the Bishop was worth trying.

His fingers moist on the phone handset, Walter explained his query to His Lordship's secretary, half-hoping that a meeting could not be granted at such short notice. He was kept waiting while a line of Beethoven's *Ode an die Freude* played in loop in the receiver (there were worse options for Easter music, he reckoned). Soon enough he was unexpectedly told that there was a free slot in the Bishop's schedule on Easter Thursday—no more than fifteen minutes though. It was too late to back down.

Three days later, ill at ease as he waited in the episcopal antechamber at Brausach that morning, the young deacon wondered yet again whether wearing his cassock rather than a mere Roman collar would not work against him. But such was the habit of his priestly community, an expression of their deep-seated sacerdotal identity. "Better show your true colours from the start," his brother Martin had advised. "You have nothing to hide. After all, the Holy Father himself wears a cassock, doesn't he?" It was too late to change anyway. Walter tried to regain hope with the thought that he had prayed his rosary at Brausach Cathedral in preparation for the meeting. Please God, the saints of the diocese would have mercy on him.

His Excellency Dr Dr Anton Braunmüller looked paternal enough in his strict charcoal grey suit and enquired about the political endeavours of Walter's brother. He had met Martin at a fundraising party for financing a water supply in Zambia.

Walter was impressed by the fact that, with his own hands, the Bishop was helping him with coffee. As the dark liquid fell into the cup, the young man looked at the broad bezel of the episcopal ring he had tried to kiss when entering the room, to His Lordship's embarrassment, it had seemed. It cost Walter to omit that ceremonial kiss at the end, while the Bishop held his coat for him to put on. Only then did His Lordship incidentally refer to Walter's First Mass. He would not mention the difficulty with *Pfarrer* Kugel, but merely expressed his hope that a solution could be found in full respect of the authority of his parish priest, a zealous and efficient pastor. Walter handed his present to His Lordship who thanked him, without opening the wrapped book yet, however. Walking quickly through the episcopal garden towards the bus station, Walter glanced at the clock and was surprised to find that he had ample time left, as the meeting had lasted less than fifteen minutes; it had felt like an hour to him.

*   *   *

Alighting from the bus back in Staufferburg, the young deacon waved faintly at a few villagers greeting him along the high street. He was not in the mood for rejoicing and, instead of walking straight home through the medieval gate, entered the *Martinskirche*. He genuflected before the baroque tabernacle and knelt down in recollection. How many times had Walter rested his elbows on this pew, on the front left side of the nave? Admittedly, one saw better from there than from the ancestral stalls in the sanctuary. Behind him, he knew, was the baptistery where he had been made a child of God, nearly thirty years earlier. In front of him, beyond the recent *Volksaltar*, at the back of the sanctuary, stood the high altar. There, his parents had been married, and his grandparents, and so on for centuries. There, he prayed to God, oh, that he might be allowed to offer his First Mass for the greater glory of the Holy Trinity, for the

living and the dead, in reparation for his sins and those of the
whole world, and in thanksgiving for so many graces he had
received from Divine Providence, in particular through his
family and his childhood spent in this cherished village!

Why was an occasion of joy for the entire community turned
into a battle? *Primiz*, the German word for First Mass, referred
to the first fruits of the harvest offered to God, after the Old
Testament stipulations. What had gone wrong? Was this opposition caused by the fact that he was not the firstborn son and
thus, not a genuine "First Fruit" for the Lord? Should his elder
brother Martin have been a priest, rather than he? Martin was
strong and clever. He would not have let himself be trapped
into this impossible situation. Even as boys, Martin would laugh
in between the paws of the colossal bear upright on its hind
legs in the Great Hall, whereas he, Walter, had never dared to
stand up to the stuffed beast (just in case, you never knew, it
was not *quite* dead).

Walter looked at the stained glass window depicting the patron
saint of his family and of the village of Staufferburg. The centu-
rion St Martin was cutting his cloak in two, covering a naked
beggar with the half which he owned as a Roman soldier, while
retaining the other half owned by the Empire. On the side wall
hung the Staufferburg coat of arms, with its familiar yellow cup
floating above a crenellated hill, as per the original meanings
of the words *Stauffer* and *Burg*. From childhood, he had been
told that the emblem represented the ceremonial cup held by
his ancestors as officials at the imperial court, resting upon
their feudal authority, symbolised by the walled hill. For the
first time though, Walter wondered if this explanation could
not be transposed to fit his priestly calling. Was he not meant
to offer up to God the chalice of salvation, transcending the
confines of his personal history and preferences to help build
the celestial Jerusalem, the heavenly city set on the mountain of
God? Suddenly, the young man felt as if the anxiety weighing

upon him for weeks was lifted: "The place is not essential! The
fruits of Mass will apply anywhere. Let me offer my First Mass
in any other church or chapel if it is God's will. May He accept
this sacrifice." Walter could not understand how such a rapid
change had occurred in his heart. It was not the result of logical
persuasion, neither was it a cowardly surrender to unjust opposition. Now he could go back to seminary for the last trimester,
peacefully awaiting the response, if any, of His Lordship.

None was sent him, and no reference was ever made to Walter's visit to Brausach either, or to his present, his book on
Baroque architecture. But *Pfarrer* Kugel soon informed him that
Dr Reich had now been requested to attend a theology seminar in
Tübingen that weekend. Deprived of his *Pastoralreferentin*, *Pfarrer*
Kugel was willing to alter the parish schedule from Eucharistic
service to Eucharistic celebration that Sunday, with Walter as the
only celebrant. The parish bulletin explained: "As many of you
are aware, Deacon Walter will be ordained a priest on Thursday
29th June in Bavaria. The Church which gathers at Staufferburg
is glad to welcome then-Father Walter for his First Mass back
home. The ceremony will take place on Sunday 8th July 2000
at 11:00am, at the *Martinskirche*, according to the pre-Conciliar
form in Latin, with kind approval from His Excellency Dr Dr
Anton Braunmüller, Bishop of Brausach. Those attending this
liturgy will fulfil the Sunday obligation. For the avoidance of
doubt, I as your shepherd confirm that Deacon Walter's priestly
Fraternity is in good standing with the Catholic Church, under
our Pope John Paul II. However, let this permission in no way
be interpreted as undermining the modern liturgical rite in force
throughout the Roman Church. We assure Deacon Walter of our
prayer as he prepares for this important occasion."

III

The Night Has Claws
(2005, ITALY)

ARRIVING BY BOAT WOULD HAVE PLEASED him more: straight to Naples, whence his father had left in 1925. But it was now 2005 and from Chile, flying a mere sixteen hours was obviously more convenient than a three-week-long crossing on an ocean liner, even when adding the surprisingly quick train journey from Rome to Benevento. Canon Manfredino De Nunzio did not feel tired. In fact, the weariness of the past few years seemed to have vanished somewhere above the Andes Mountains, as if he were a couple of decades younger, at the time of his first appointment as Parish Priest at Santa Isabel, that dull-looking little church at the bottom of *Calle Olmos*. How far away Valparaíso now felt! Next to him on the back seat of the taxi, his young cousin Pedro was the one who was asleep (dreaming no *pesadilla*, judging from his happy features), as Pietrelcina disappeared behind a hill.

Canon Manfredino had liked the little town in hilly Campania. *Pietrelcina . . .* To think that it had taken him sixty-four years to visit the family place for the first time! He was no expert in Italian cuisine and the restaurant run by his relatives seemed a modest affair (but the downstairs lavatory was immaculate and tastefully tiled: he would award it four stars). The "cousins" had been welcoming enough, not making him feel too much of a stranger despite his very basic Italian. What had worked in his favour was that, unlike many pilgrims claiming some vague connection with the saint, he was truly related to Padre Pio. The grandfather of the stigmatist priest was Fortunato De Nunzio, whose cousins Luigi and Antonio had emigrated to Chile. In Valparaíso, Luigi had married Canon Manfredino's mother, while Uncle Antonio had remained single for a while, until he joined a Carmelite monastery. People prayed in Latin in those days, so that Uncle Antonio's nonexistent Spanish had not barred him from becoming a friar in Chile.

Reluctantly, Canon Manfredino admitted that keeping the family *trattoria* in Pietrelcina made no sense. "Why would I, a busy canon lawyer in the diocese of Valparaíso, own a house in Italy, twelve thousand kilometres away from home?" Sure, his father had been born in that old house on Via Riella, as had his grandfather. When he was a child, the black-and-white photographs of the faraway village would shine before his eyes as a paradise lost, in the yellowing family album. The picture with "Uncle" Pio himself and his father and cousins as young men, taken in the 1920s, was considered a family relic. (It was now taped, the Canon recalled with embarrassment, since as a toddler he had once impatiently pulled the precious photo from his mother's hand and accidentally torn it in two.) In the 1960s, when more pilgrims started visiting the hometown of Padre Pio, their relatives had turned the house into a business. His father had agreed to let out the property to them. His death five months earlier had left Canon Manfredino the sole heir (in his Carmel, childless Uncle Antonio had renounced all claims to this inheritance). The Canon's mind was set on selling—although surely not to that American couple of Pio devotees who had been pestering him during supper the night before: no, he had never met Padre Pio and again no, he had never lived in Pietrelcina—and never would!

Canon Manfredino had a different plan. *Pedro* would inherit! It was officially for the sake of company that he had invited his young cousin to join him on that trip to Italy. The lad had no Italian connection, since he was on the Canon's mother's side, that is, a Chilean through and through. But there was that lovely girl, Tina, from La Calera, a town in the mountainous hinterland. The Canon hoped she would not be radicalised by the so called "pro-life" movement. She'd even asked *him* — Canon Manfredino, a doctor in canon Law — if he would attend their prayer vigil outside an abortion clinic! And what of his reputation? Mind you, the girl was persuasive and he'd nearly agreed. She was hoping to qualify as midwife and would come to his church in Valparaíso by bus every fortnight — when Pedro was around. Canon Manfredino smiled as he recalled how, unintentionally, he had surprised the couple in the presbytery kitchen two months earlier. He had allowed Pedro to gather an informal youth group at his parish. The young people would share a meal and he would give a little talk on any topic they liked. Strangely, they had more time for theology than for football, forgetting that the very first football club in Chile had been started in Valparaíso. So much for ancestral traditions! That evening in the sitting-room, the animated discussion ran on the old rules of Eucharistic fast. Most youngsters wished the Church would bring back the three-hour fast, if not the midnight one. Why not the old Ember Days, while these hotheads were at it!

But Tina was taking longer time than expected to bring coffee and cakes from the kitchen, so that Canon Manfredino had discreetly come to enquire. As he had walked along the corridor, he had overheard Pedro's voice from the kitchen, first hushed, and then clearly thrilled: "To Valparaíso? You've been accepted! I can't believe it! So, you'll be next door!" The Canon had stopped, embarrassed, while Tina's voice, altogether shy and firm, had answered: "That's our dream come true, Pedro, thank God. We should tell our families, soon." The priest had cleared his throat to make his presence known before gently pushing the door open. Before him, with an ecstatic smile on his face, Pedro was still holding Tina's left hand, while with her right one she was quickly trying to brush tears from her hazel eyes. The Canon had asked no question, of course — the girl's blushing cheeks provided the answer. But lying in bed that evening, his somehow weary heart had felt rejuvenated. How long had those two been

courting (was that the right word for modern youths going out
together)? Pedro had concealed his interest well, but he could
not have made a better choice. What a lovely bride Tina would
look! Yes, he could picture the handsome couple Pedro and
Tina would make, and was looking forward to baptising their
children. But before that, he, Uncle Fredi, would buy a flat in
the city for the impecunious young pair. There would be a lift,
for the pram. Unless a Ground Floor flat were better, with a
small garden for the children to play in. Oh no! Children get
kidnapped in precisely such gardens, like last year in Santiago.
First things first. Whether Ground- or First Floor, he could
buy no flat without cash, hence the sale of the Italian *trattoria*.

If it hadn't been for Pedro, he might have waited a bit longer
before making a decision. He liked what he had seen of Italy since
their arrival two days earlier. Through the taxi window, these
bushy mounds looked like mere molehills compared with the
Andes, back home. But there was charm in small scale. The car
should reach San Giovanni Rotondo within an hour, hopefully.
He noticed that Pedro's hands were actually busy with rosary
beads. So, the boy was not asleep, despite keeping his eyes shut.
A nice little fellow, he was, despite his awkward love for the old
Latin Mass. Where had the lad heard about it anyway? Nowhere
near Valparaíso was it ever celebrated. Or could he have discovered Uncle Antonio's little secret (just as he, Manfredino, had
found out the young man's sweetheart)? Yes, that was plausible.
Uncle Antonio had permission from his superior to use the
nearly extinct Carmelite rite of Mass, behind locked doors. His
young cousin might even have served the old priest's lonely Mass,
down in the friary crypt. There was nothing the Canon could do
about it. Youngsters like to contradict their parents. Pedro had
just embraced the old Latin Mass like his elders had taken pride
in television, contraception and Liberation Theology. Would the
next generation cancel the internet and possibly revert to the
telegraph? Well, he would be long gone by then.

Canon Manfredino knew that he was being insincere. Deep inside, he was feeling increasingly attracted to this perplexing old Latin Mass. But why had his sick father asked for his funeral to be celebrated in that antiquated form? Was the Novus Ordo in Latin not good enough? As a senior priest in his diocese he got away with a more conservative way of offering Mass. Unlike his fellow parish priest at San Felipe, he'd never denied anyone Communion on the tongue, for instance. His old man had not made the traditional Requiem a strict command. He had simply expressed a wish, "If it is not inconvenient for you Fredi, because it was what I grew up with and it would be a bit like dying at home, back in Pietrelcina." A good son, Canon Manfredino had tried to learn the ancient Mass. Or rather, to speak the truth, he *had* learned it, and quicker than expected. But five months later, when his father had eventually passed away as peacefully as his cancer allowed, the new bishop had just been appointed. He was a former canon law student of Manfredino's and . . . Well, there were not many men able to take over as Vicar General, were there? But whoever would be chosen would have to be wise; some would say *political*. Was it his fault, Canon Manfredino moaned inwardly, if the more influential clerics around him saw the old Latin Mass as divisive? And was he not obligated to his diocese to foster harmony for the common good?

Everybody had praised the dignity of the funeral service. He had made a point in wearing purple vestments rather than white, and he'd managed to dispense with altar girls since young Pedro, a close relative to the deceased, had conveniently stepped in. He had used the Roman Canon, with its lengthy enumeration of saints which his father particularly liked. He had respected the old man's wish for a burial, rather than cremation; and for his cherished Campanian canticle to the *Madonna della Libera* to be sung during the Offertory by a professional choir (at a cost). So, what more could have been done? Canon Manfredino's eyes caught sight again of Pedro's fingers holding the

rosary beads. The wooden spheres moved very slowly from one
hand to the next. Good, a young man who prays the Madonna.
The priest looked at his watch. Leaning towards the driver, he
asked alternatively in Spanish and English: "Are we still far? I
would need to stop. Toilet, you understand *toilet*?"—but to no
avail. Then, opening his Italian guidebook he uttered, "*Dov'è
il bagno per favore?*"

After a break demanded by the Canon's aging body, the taxi
finally came in sight of San Giovanni Rotondo. Canon Manfredino was glad to see the place where his saintly relative had
received such extraordinary graces from God. For decades, Uncle
Pio had borne the marks of Christ's Five Wounds on his own
limbs and chest, a phenomenon medically verified but scientif-
ically unexplained. The saint had also been known to bilocate,
as formally testified by witnesses who had seen him in distant
places at the same time. And what of that US Air Force pilot
during the Second World War, who was about to drop bombs
on a German target in Southern Italy, when a Capuchin friar of
colossal proportions had appeared before his jet, high in the sky,
gesturing that this location was to be spared? The pilot had no
idea who the monk was (let alone how he could fly) until years
later he met Padre Pio and recognised him. As if this was not
enough, Uncle Pio was known to converse with angels and to
fight devils. Speaking of angels, Canon Manfredino's guidebook
mentioned that a car ride away uphill was the very ancient shrine
to Archangel St Michael on Mount Gargano. No doubt, this was
a part of the world where supernatural battles had been fought,
and perhaps still were. The Canon suddenly felt a bit wanting
by contrast with his extraordinary uncle. What battles had *he*,
Manfredino, fought, or won? What of his pastoral undertak-
ings? What of his own sanctification? He was not a great sinner,
admittedly. But had he any zeal left? San Giovanni Rotondo was
renowned as a place to go to confession. Canon Manfredino
decided that he would avail himself of it.

Lunch at the hotel was light enough, and the red wine happened to be a Chilean *Carmenere*, much to Pedro's taste; the Canon abstained, preferring water. In fact, Canon Manfredino found that his body required less and less food and drink as he grew older. But young men like Pedro needed calories, so that the priest ordered extra sides for him. He felt like teasing his young cousin a bit: "Why boy do you want to stick to the old Latin Mass—or rather, why come back to it—when even the only stigmatist priest went along with the new Mass in Italian? See, on this picture, Padre Pio is saying Mass facing the people. The altar stands between him and the congregation." Pedro looked at the guidebook and after a while suggested: "Uncle Fredi, this picture was taken before Pope Paul VI's new Mass. The caption states that Uncle Pio died on September 23, 1968, whereas the new missal came in force in 1970 only."

The boy was right, he recalled, since he, Manfredino, had been ordained a subdeacon the year Uncle Pio had died. This realisation upset the Canon. Not that it changed anything, really. After all, Padre Pio would probably have said the new Mass if he had lived. So, why should it affect him, a distant relative in a faraway country? Undeniably however, he was slightly annoyed at God for having called Uncle Pio back before the new Missal went in force, as if it was unfair that the Capuchin stigmatist should have been spared the ... —spared *what*, exactly? Changing his mind, Canon Manfredino helped himself to a first glass of red. He knew that the difficulties of his priestly ministry weighed very little compared with the sufferings endured by his saintly uncle: the open wounds of the stigmatisation, and the persecution by his Capuchin superiors, forbidding him for several years to meet with the throngs of pilgrims, because they were jealous of his pastoral fame and bitter to see the vast alms he was channelling to his state-of-the-art hospital, named by him "The House to Alleviate Suffering." He would have liked to meet Padre Pio, a man of integrity and sacrifice. He, a doctor in canon law and

a respected official in his diocese of Valparaíso, felt he would
have dared to ask the Capuchin, as a little boy his father, what
it meant to be a priest and what was the most important thing a
priest must do. He knew the answers, but he felt not sufficiently
at peace to hear them, except from a saint and an uncle.

Was it the bill? Not yet. The waiter was visibly expecting
them to order some desserts. Why not after all? Canon Manfredino reverted to less challenging considerations and unad-
venturously chose tiramisus, with Pedro's approval. "The name
of that cake means 'Pull-me-up,' my guidebook says. I wonder
why." Unexpectedly, the thought of his forthcoming confession
crossed his mind, with the vague hope that it would pull him
up spiritually. As he awaited their last course, he wondered if
now was not a good occasion to break the news of the flat to
Pedro. Why keep the dear boy in financial uncertainty, when his
matrimonial plans demanded security? He would be straightforward. "Pedro, I have something to tell you. I have decided
to sell the family *trattoria* in Pietrelcina. But the money will
stay in the family. I will buy you a flat in Valparaíso and you
can move in with Tina." He paused, relishing the astonishment
on his cousin's juvenile face.

"What do you mean, Uncle Fredi?"

"Come on boy: don't think me naïve. You obviously love each
other. She's a good girl. I have some money and no children,
while you will want children but have no money. So, I will help
you both start a family. Since you can't afford a place, I give
one to you. Simple, no?"

"But Uncle Fredi, we are not in love—and she's about to
become a nun."

"What! Don't pull my leg, kid, I heard Tina the other night
saying she was moving to Valparaíso, and she wanted you to
tell your families about your wedding plans."

"Ah? When you found us in the kitchen? Uncle, you misun-
derstood us. She had just been admitted to a traditional Carmel

in the U. S. A. The place is in the middle of nowhere though, in a village called Valparaíso, Nebraska."

Canon Manfredino was deeply confused. But he suddenly remembered a detail in the previous conversation. Inquisitorially, he stated: "Pedro, I heard you answer her that you would be neighbours, or something to that effect. And by the way, I was not eavesdropping. So, why deny your marriage plans any further?"

The young man looked pensive and embarrassed. Canon Manfredino felt he had hit home. No more tricks: his young cousin would have to admit the truth. Pedro breathed deeply and answered:

"Uncle Fredi, I am entering seminary in September. I am on my way to becoming a priest. And the place where I was accepted, by God's providence, is in Nebraska, half an hour from Tina's Carmel."

*   *   *

Standing in the queue outside the only confessional displaying the sign "Spanish," Canon Manfredino was doing his best to focus on his examination of conscience. But like a disobedient dog playing with his master's empty slipper, his mind was stubbornly biting again and again at the devastating news he had just heard from Pedro. He knew he ought to avoid the topic until he cooled down. But it was beyond his power. He was hurt, but that was not the worst. Deep down, he was afraid; afraid of being left alone — or left *behind*. The prospect of being associated with this young couple whom he loved as their childless uncle had kept him going. But he was now the last one standing in his generation, and fellow clergy were not exactly like family. "Ah yes, I still have Uncle Antonio. Speak of the devil! Surely this was his doing. He must have put these strange ideas in the impressionable heads of Pedro and Tina. Why should they go and seek *his* opinion in the first place, an old recluse friar, when they could have asked me anything and benefitted from my pastoral and canonical experience? But never once did they request my advice—I was just good enough to lend my presbytery for their radical youth parties!"

Canon Manfredino stopped brooding for a while, realising that he now would need to add resentment and jealousy to the list of sins for his forthcoming confession. There were three penitents left ahead of him in the queue and it was barely 4pm. He might even try to offer Mass after that, albeit on his own. Admittedly, there was no pastoral need since he was on holiday, but San Giovanni Rotondo was a special place for priests. That prospect having pacified him a little, he allowed his thoughts to shift again to the revelation just heard from his young cousin. At least, why not apply to the *diocesan* seminary in Valparaíso, if Pedro had to be a priest? While Tina also could have joined the Nurses of St Joseph. They were nuns whose confessions he heard on occasion. They were desperate for young women to apply before their community were all in wheel chairs and needing nursing rather than providing it. Was it not selfish, somehow, to desert their home city, their country, and escape to the U. S. in some posh and radical new communities? Why was it that those new places attracted the millions of dollars and the young people? Canon Manfredino cast away the far-fetched vision of a haughty Mother Prioress landing in a white helicopter at her marble Carmel, surrounded by hundreds of young sisters. Trying to be objective, he recalled Pedro's assurance that he had not meant to apply to a seminary so close to where Tina would live. He had wished to enter instead that community's other seminary in Europe. But Uncle Antonio—he again!—had told him that it made more sense to remain on the American side of the Atlantic. While Pedro spoke no German, his English was acceptable; and he would never get to see the strictly enclosed Carmelite nuns "next door" anyway. The place had to be surrounded with grilles!

"Still two penitents waiting. This is worse than at the Central Post Office, back home." Unable to ignore any longer a pressing natural need, Canon Manfredino reluctantly left his place in the confession queue. Alas, the cleaning lady kept him waiting outside the shrine lavatory while she refreshed the place, so that on his hasty return the Spanish sign was off above the confessional and the Spanish-speaking penitents gone. It was the last straw. This time, he let his anger out, admonishing in his heart Uncle Padre Pio now up in heaven: "You know I cannot confess properly in Italian. You drag hundreds of foreigners here daily to be absolved in their native tongue, and you leave me, your own kinsman, without assistance! What is worse, you must have known all along that these two little rascals were plotting to let me down, me and the Church in Chile, to run away to the Yanks; and you let me set up plans and make a fool of myself, offering them a flat they care less about than their last *curanto al hoyo*! What is so special about this old Latin Mass anyway? Why are these young people flocking to it? Tina's place gets dozens of applicants every year, Pedro boasted to me, and they have now two daughter monasteries. In his blind enthusiasm, the lad was so insensitive as to suggest they might soon found another house . . . in *Chile*. Indeed? Who says we, the Church in Chile, would welcome those radical inexperienced holier-than-thou sisters? Is sanctity measured by the length of one's veil or cassock; or by the hours spent kneeling, or by how fast one can read Latin?" The diatribe ended as Canon Manfredino realised that his own Latin was not bad at all. A bit less upset, he made his way towards the main church.

A paradoxical thought occurred to him, suddenly, as he wandered towards the crypt where Uncle Pio lay buried. Yes, he would show them that it didn't matter to him. They would see that he was able to do it when he pleased. After all, he had practised long enough until his . . . Until his father's death; even though he had never actually said an old rite Mass, for

real. Well, now he would. There and then. Surely, there would
be an old missal for him to use, tucked somewhere in the
sacristy drawers. Possibly, but the responses: who would make
them? He would not ask Pedro. He really did not feel composed
enough to have him around on that occasion. But of course,
he simply would offer a Requiem Mass! At old rite Masses
for the dead, he recalled, the long impossible dialogue at the
beginning was skipped, so that he would not need to worry
about responses at all. He would walk up to the altar in no
time, and from then on would simply read the Latin words
from the missal and the altar cards. Altar cards? Bother, where
would he find altar cards, these framed prayers to be displayed
on the altar for reading outside the missal? If he was lucky
enough to get his hands on an old rite missal, digging up altar
cards in addition might be asking for too much. Or else, let
that be Uncle Pio's job. Yes, let him provide what was needed,
if it made any difference. Failure would be his answer. Uncle
Pio was well-known for extraordinary signs and favours. Let
he tell his kinsman whether or not saying that old rite Latin
Mass was relevant in modern times.

Canon Manfredino had assumed that he would be led to
the main altar in the church. Instead, he was surprised to be
directed to a private chapel inside the friary. On entering the
plain room with its whitewashed rugged walls, its high vaulted
ceiling and narrow grilled window, he felt as if his anger, disappointment and anxiety were gently washed away by some
invisible tide. The door was shut behind him before he could
remember to ask about the old rite items. Strangely, it did not
matter so much to him anymore. Feeling tired, though not
weary, he sat on a low wooden stool, letting his gaze meet the
wide Italian crucifix above the small altar set against the wall.
There was love and quiet in that room; perhaps even a hint of
fatherly humour, unexpectedly. Only after a few months had
passed, looking back, would he be able to define the change

that had occurred in his soul. It could be expressed in one word: "home." Something very deep in him felt fulfilled, almost unnoticeably. After five minutes, he started setting up for Mass. Sure enough, a side cupboard yielded an ancient tome whose binding bore the barely discernible gilded title *Missale Romanum Seraphicum*. It had been printed in 1925.

Requiem aeternam dona eis Domine: et lux perpetua luceat eis. The beginning of the Mass sounded very familiar. Yes, *Eternal rest give to them O Lord; and let perpetual light shine upon them.* Canon Manfredino knew whom in particular he would offer this Mass for. "How does one say *Luigi* in Latin, and what ending should it be: *Ludovico*? That would have to do." *Kyrie, eleison! Kyrie, eleison! Kyrie, eleison!* Three times Lord have mercy? He was glad that his attention had to be applied to saying the Mass in progress rather than probe his conscience. And yet, like a bullet extracted from some vital organ of a semi-conscious wounded man, the confession he had until then not dared to utter was articulated for him, as if by an angel at his side: "Human respect deterred me from offering the old rite Requiem my father had hoped for." That was it. He had not even felt pain when admitting to the guilt he had ignored for months. But he presently experienced a liberating sorrow. Oh no, that he might not weep now, at his age! To contain his emotion, he forced himself to focus on the epistle: *I heard a voice from heaven saying to me: Write: Blessed are the dead, who die in the Lord. From henceworth now, saith the Spirit, that they may rest from their labours, for their works follow them.* How incredibly hard his old man had worked, for sure, Canon Manfredino recalled. "Please, dear God, may he now rest from his many labours, from his sweat and sorrows on my behalf."

After the Gospel, when pivoting to say *Dominus vobiscum*, Canon Manfredino jumped as he caught sight of Pedro, on his knees a few steps away. How had the lad got in there, and so quietly? But there was no time to ask, of course, and the priest

carried on offering the Mass. The Offertory rites went well,
even without a procession of gifts. Instead, Pedro spontaneously
presented the cruets and the Lavabo bowl. Canon Manfredino
felt almost happy to have the young man involved (despite his
marriage betrayal). The Preface was very eloquent and after the
Sanctus, Canon Manfredino knew that the holiest part of the
Mass was about to begin. In the old rite, the Eucharistic Prayer
had to be said entirely in silence. There would be no turning
back to the people, no eye contact of any kind but instead, a
radical focusing on the Sacrifice of Christ about to be renewed
on that little altar. The Canon turned the page, and saw...

What the hell was this! The first page of the Eucharistic Prayer
was lacerated to the point of illegibility. How strange... It
was not a mere scratch. In fact there were three — no — four
long furrows running parallel all across the page, diagonally.
They ended before the edge though, so that the sheet still held
together. Canon Manfredino paused for a moment since the
tearing prevented further reading; but also out of perplexity.
Who could have damaged the Missal in this peculiar way?
Could it have been an accident? A child might have teasingly
left his mark, as surely no adult would find this funny. But
children's hands are not that wide. Why should it be a *human*
limb after all? The four marks could have been left by claws,
rather than fingernails. After all, Franciscans like pets. Perhaps
the dog at the friary got shut up by mistake in this room and
in desperation jumped on the altar, damaging the Missal. But,
Canon Manfredino realised, this book would never lay open
on the altar unless a priest were standing there, offering Mass.
Only then did another explanation furtively cross the mind of
the canon. He tried to ignore it because it was farfetched — but
also because it was frightening. Reluctantly, he admitted that
there was in fact a possibility, however unbelievable, that the
claws were not of this world. He shivered slightly, a sensation
of *grima* catching his heart as when in his schoolboy years

he heard the detestable sound of fingernails on a blackboard.

By then, Pedro was standing next to him, enquiring as to why his uncle would not proceed with the prayers. He saw the lacerated page and both men looked at each other in silence. Canon Manfredino decided to move on: "Too bad for the Roman Canon. I will use the Prayer Eucharistic Number Two instead." As he started flickering through the Missal, Pedro whispered: "Uncle Fredi, there are no several Eucharistic Prayers in the traditional Missal. The Roman Canon is the only one available." Canon Manfredino had forgotten. Pedro left the altar and took out of his bag a red booklet, which he handed open to the Canon: "It's my old server's guidebook, from Uncle Antonio, with the Latin text of the Mass on the left pages and the Spanish text on the right ones. I can set it on the missal stand for you to read from." So it was done. By then, Canon Manfredino did not even mind the mention of his Carmelite Uncle, the stubborn traditionalist. After all, his booklet would prove useful. The Mass ended without further incident. The Canon was proud to have remembered *not* to give the final blessing omitted at Requiem Masses, and to say *Requiescant in pace* instead of the customary *Ite missa est*.

* * *

A few months later, in the middle of Advent, he was smiling on his way back from the bank. They had confirmed to him that the first transaction had gone through. He was old school (meaning "not computer literate"), and rather than doing it himself online, he had asked his local branch to check with the Italian bank that his instructions had been carried out. The family *trattoria* at Pietrelcina had not been sold after all. Instead, the monthly rent was sent from Italy by the Pietrelcina cousins directly to Nebraska. It covered most of Pedro's formation fees at his traditional seminary. Canon Fredi was invited for the Tonsure ceremony the following autumn, when a bishop would cut five chunks of Pedro's hair and formally clothe him with the black cassock and white surplice, along with his eighteen other classmates, please God.

That was all very well, but he could not accept the invitation, having found the previous trip to Italy more tiring than anticipated. More to the point, he dreaded the scrutiny of these highly trained traditional clerics. They would watch him like hawks as he would clumsily try to set the biretta on his head with three fingers at Vespers (although he had practised, standing before his bedroom mirror) and would guess within seconds that he was not the genuine article. Might they not laugh at him? And what if pictures of him in such a surrounding were posted on the Internet for his fellow priests to criticise back in Valparaíso? After all, why would he go to such lengths (alienating his long-time friends in the deanery in addition) for a priestly style which was not really his thing? As his bus arrived to take him back to his part of town, he felt relieved not to fly to Nebraska.

Sitting down, he took out of his breast pocket the envelope with the address of Tina's parents. They had failed to make him change his mind. The girl was thriving, they wrote, as a Carmelite novice in *Valparaíso*. ("Or so-called by the Yanks: how dared they name a Nebraskan hamlet after our glorious Chilean harbour, with our National Congress and seven universities!") But her parents could not afford flying to Nebraska when their daughter would receive the Carmelite habit and veil, planned three weeks before Pedro's Tonsure the following autumn, if all went well. Would he agree to deliver to her at the Carmel a framed holy picture and some Chilean delicacies to share with the community as presents? If brought by a fellow-Chilean, the parents' letter pleaded, and by a priest who also had supported their daughter in her vocation (Canon Fredi remembered that he'd rather wished her to become Pedro's wife!), the gifts would touch Tina much more than if sent by post. Happily annoyed by the request, the Canon had written back that he was unable to attend the ceremony, while Chilean food would not be allowed through American customs. Stepping out of the bus, he slipped in a mailbox the envelope with his response to Tina's parents, admitting to himself that he had liked the suggestion of acting as ambassador from the motherland to a deserving young woman. Did his surname not mean "nuncio" after all? Of course, he had insisted, he would pray for the two young adults and would "celebrate the Eucharist" for their intentions.

Canon Manfredino was decidedly in a good mood that morning. He felt a free man, immune from accidental influences while acting charitably on his own terms. The weather was pleasantly warm and he untied his scarf as he reached *Calle Olmos*, with his bleak-looking Santa Isabel Church. "A fortnight to Christmas," he thought, "and the crib is not ready yet in the St Pio side chapel." But that would wait, as he was on his day off and the visit to the bank that morning was enough business done. He stepped into the church, finding it empty as he expected. As every Tuesday, Padre Miguel from San Felipe had kindly offered the 9 o'clock parish Mass for him (within 23 minutes, including homily and Communion). He genuflected and walked straight into the sacristy. Padre Miguel's fedora hat and sports scarf (bearing the Santiago Wanderers football club's green and white emblem!) still lay on the vestment press. "He must have left in a hurry," Canon Fredi surmised.

He set the cruets and missal for his private Mass on the side altar in St Pio's Chapel, concealed behind the eight-feet-high starry paper backdrop of the Christmas crib. With annoyance, he noticed that the sacristan had *still* not sellotaped the painted paper sheets torn the previous year. On its outer side, the Bethlehem houses and hills looked disjointed, as if after some earthquake. How many times was he to remind his lay assistant to complete such a simple task? No, he would not

mend it himself—or not now, not on his day off! Having lit the
candles, he took a last look at the altar. Was everything on it
ready? No need for the tabernacle key, of course. As this Mass
was purposely unannounced, there would be no server and
no congregation. "Just as well," he admitted. There was barely
enough space for the celebrant to stand between the Christmas
screen and the little altar. The sacristy clock confirmed that his
breakfast had been ingested nearly three hours earlier. Canon
law demanded a one-hour fast only before Communion, but
he was glad to extend it when possible. He washed his hands
and started vesting. Having tied the chasuble around his waist,
he signed himself and bowed to the crucifix on the wall. When
walking out of the sacristy though, he remembered that he
had omitted to lock the church door as was his custom when
saying Mass alone. "Bother! And what if Miguel turns up to
fetch his scarf and cap, and sees me wearing these? I will be a
marked man in the deanery..." Instinctively, his right fingers
came to feel the item loosely hanging across his left wrist—a
maniple—(his left hand still holding the chalice). Should he
walk to the front door and lock it, he wondered, unconsciously
pushing the incriminatory band of cloth against his sleeve?

But it was too late; someone had just slammed the church
door. As anticipated, the heavy footsteps of his fellow priest
were coming his way, no doubt aiming for the sacristy. Canon
Fredi tensed up as he stood still between the side altar and the
Christmas screen, spying on the bulky silhouette through the
torn paper backdrop. "What a ridiculous situation," he groaned
within, "now I am made to feel like a delinquent in my own
church!" Keeping silent in his hiding place, he waited for Padre
Miguel to collect his belongings and leave, wishing that the
flames of the lit candles would not attract his visitor's attention to the hidden side-altar. Soon enough any sound ceased;
and yet, the church door had not been opened or shut. Glancing again in perplexity through the tear in the crib paper, his

fingers moist around the foot of the gilded chalice, Canon Fredi caught a most unexpected sight. Thinking himself unseen in the empty church, Padre Miguel was now prostrate in the central aisle, facing the tabernacle! "What? I never saw him display any such reverence towards the Holy Eucharist. Why does he keep his love secret?"

The church door was finally slammed again and Canon Fredi was able to take a deep breath. He had not been caught; not this time. He took off his biretta, set the vessel on the altar and opened the missal before coming down the step to begin his Mass. As he was about to whisper the first words, he had a faint sensation of a presence nearby. But no sound confirmed his sentiment. "Of course," he smiled, "the Lord is in the tabernacle, on the high altar." Reassured, he eventually uttered: *Introibo ad altare Dei* .... Meanwhile, by the door at the far rear of the nave, inconspicuous on his knees, his *Santiago Wanderers* green scarf hanging around his neck, Padre Miguel would probably not have known the response: *Ad Deum qui laetificat juventutem meam*. But through the torn starry paper of the crib-in-progress in the Padre Pio chapel, his eyes did not notice the flickering candles. At least, he never referred to it afterwards.

Bastille Day

(2001, FRANCE)

"LAFAYETTE, HERE WE ARE!" ROBBIE SMILED with childlike satisfaction as he set foot on French soil at Charles-De-Gaulle airport in Paris. His dream was becoming reality—at last he was visiting the native land of freedom, the heroic nation whence human rights had spread across the Atlantic and shaped his own country, "the land of the free and the home of the brave." Standing near the shuttle stop to the city centre, his eyes shut, he inhaled the humid Parisian air. It was not as hot as in Philadelphia though, despite it being already 13th July. A youthful face with a Roman collar grinned at him, reflected on the glass of the bus door. No, he did not look 28 at all, more like 25. To think that less than a year earlier he was just Deacon Robbie—and seven years previous, Ensign Edgworth, of the U.S. Coast Guards.

It was kind of Dave to have asked him to preach at his wedding (for the sake of the many English-speakers in the congregation). After all, they had almost lost touch with each other since Robbie had left the Coast Guards in his fourth year. It brought back memories of tough times at Training Center Cape May when he, Dave, Mike, Sam, and Pete were raw recruits—memories of rough seas and of strong brotherhood. Dave was now a Lieutenant Commander and about to be married (Mike acting as Best Man), while Robbie had been a priest for over a year in Philadelphia, memorably ordained on 1st July 2000, only three days before Independence Day. Robbie didn't know Stéphanie, apart from the fact that she was Catholic and French (that sounded promising). Friends of her parents, the Lembert family, had offered him to stay in their flat, which Robbie now easily found "right behind the U. S. embassy," as

Dave had mentioned. Robbie was thrilled to discover that the
building stood along the Champs-Élysées where the traditional
military parade would take place the following morning, on
Bastille Day.

Pointing his finger through the open window, his host
Mr Lembert told Robbie that in winter one could see the
Champs-Élysées through the leafless chestnut trees. "Right across,
over there; no, not to the right: these are the Japanese and the
British embassies, and right to the end, the Élysée Palace."

"Where President Chirac lives?" Robbie enquired.

"So I am told," Mr Lembert replied as if not particularly *au
fait*. He was a dignified but unassuming elderly man with a
very gentle manner about him, wearing a neat three-piece pale
blue suit of outmoded cut, and a tie.

Robbie longed to watch the various French regiments marching down from the *Arc de Triomphe* to the *Place de la Concorde*. He was particularly keen to see the Republican Guard,
the last mounted regiment in the French armed forces. It had
been somehow started by Napoleon he recalled, that other
great Frenchman. With striking humility though, Mr Lembert
remarked that Bonaparte was more Corsican than French; while
the oldest French military unit was actually the *Gendarmerie*,
dating back to the *Ancien Régime*. "Will the French *Garde-Côtes*
march as well?" Robbie asked. He had met some in the West
Indies, at the Gustavia training session in Saint-Barthelemy. But
to the young priest's dismay, Mr Lembert replied that he never
watched the Bastille Day parade, although he had once been part
of it, after World War II. (Really, could Mr Lembert be *that* old?)

Not for the first time since taking off the previous day, the
question of missing the 14th July parade pricked Robbie's conscience. As a former Naval Officer he took legitimate interest
in such a significant military event; and as an American patriot,
how could he miss Bastille Day, when the invention of freedom was commemorated? But as a priest and a friend of the

bridegroom, his priority should be to offer his Mass and make his way to the church where the wedding was to take place as early as 11:00am. Why did it have to clash with the parade, Robbie moaned! Why not get married in the afternoon?

To make things worse, since a Baptism was scheduled in that church right before the wedding, Dave had insisted that there would be just enough time to set up for the ceremony, and definitely no chance for Robbie to offer Mass there in private before the nuptial one. The latter could not be concelebrated either, as it is apparently not the custom for traditional Latin Masses. If Robbie had known that older rite, Dave obligingly added, of course he could have done the wedding Mass itself. It had been finally agreed that Robbie would ask the local parish of St Madeleine instead, which opened at 8:30am, near the Lemberts' flat. But that would leave him barely an hour after his Mass to watch the military parade, roughly between 9:15am and 10:15am. Robbie's last hope vanished when Mr Lembert suggested: "The parade begins at 10:00am. Do take an umbrella, if you are interested in attending, as it will surely rain. You might see the beginning before getting to the church for the wedding. We are going to the country this afternoon for the anniversary of my wife's ancestor tomorrow, but Elvira, our old housekeeper, will take care of you. Meanwhile, if you are not too jetlagged, would you care to accompany me to St Madeleine Church, so that you don't get lost on your way to say your Mass tomorrow morning? The parish priest told me that you would be welcome."

Shortly after 5pm, Robbie followed his host out of the flat's ancient courtyard. On either side of the *Rue du Faubourg-St-Honoré*, elegant passers-by and fashion industry staff were waiting behind safety barriers. Robbie enquired whether the Republican Guard from the nearby Élysée Palace was per-haps rehearsing for the parade the following day. A hundred armoured horsemen would need the entire street cleared, especially if holding sabres! But at that moment, the crowd (and Mr Lembert) burst into joyful shouting: "*Vive la Reine! Vive la Reine!*" Visibly pleased with the occasion, Mr Lembert obligingly translated:

"Long live the Queen! Look Fr Robbie, Her Majesty!" Before Robbie's doubtful eyes, a long convertible Bentley State limousine glided through the archway of the British Embassy. Sitting at the back, faintly waving gloved hands, an old couple graced the throng with regal smiles and vanished. Robbie could not believe that he had just seen the English Queen — Elizabeth II, was it not — and her Prince Consort. Gee! When he would tell them about it, back home! He had felt like waving and shouting together with the enthusiastic crowd, but had suddenly remembered that his country had heroically won its independence from that very monarchy. He restrained his excitement. However, he then realised, were not all these keen onlookers supposed to be dutiful citizens of the French Republic? How could they cheer a *queen* — and just a few yards away from the presidential palace? Were they not taking chances with freedom; or at least, did their feudal enthusiasm not contradict the determination of their ancestors at the French Revolution? Robbie looked at them more carefully as Mr Lembert led him across the street towards *Sainte Madeleine* Church. This was the heart of the Fashion District, surrounded with luxury boutiques bearing names he had distractedly noticed in the inflight magazine before landing: *Yves Saint Laurent, Hermès, Givenchy, Dior, Chanel . . .* It did not seem a particularly monarchist area, not as if nostalgists of the *Ancien Régime* had gathered there on purpose that afternoon just to greet a foreign monarch. On the contrary, the crowd looked very trendy and rather young, holding no fleur-de-lys flags and wearing no powdered wigs, apparently. How to account for their enthusiasm, then? Walking across *Rue Royale* towards *Sainte Madeleine*, Robbie concluded that freedom was perhaps a more complex issue than he had imagined.

* * *

That evening, the young priest hesitantly took out of his suitcase his Coast Guard uniform and spread it upon his bed. He had never worn it since entering seminary. But Mike, Dave's Best Man, had insisted that for old times' sake the five of them, former fellow cadets at Training Center Cape May, should wear their uniforms for Dave's bachelor party. Persuasively, Mike had promised to get Robbie a chaplain's emblem to pin on his lapel, to show that he was attending as a priest friend, not as a Coast Guard. That is how Robbie found himself walking along *Place de la Concorde* at 8pm, looking a Coast Guard Ensign once again, on his way to the bank of the Seine where the bridegroom was to be treated to a Prestige dinner cruise. Upon reaching the *Champs-Élysées*, Robbie stood for a few minutes on the narrow traffic island, waiting for the pedestrian crossing light to turn green. Uphill, in the distance, he could see the gigantic silhouette of the *Arc de Triomphe*, while in the opposite direction the Louvre Museum spread its wings towards the majestic *Place de la Concorde*. To think that he could have been marching right there the following morning among the various foreign representatives, at the military parade...

"Welcome aboard!" Robbie was thrilled to set foot on the *Edith Piaf*, a large vessel with panoramic windows to watch the legendary Paris monuments along either bank. He greeted his former fellow Coast Guards bridegroom Dave, Mike the Best Man, plus Sam and Pete his "back-on-the-block" buddies freshly landed from America like him. The five men then followed the steward into the navigation bridge, which was oddly set at the bow. There, the group was warmly greeted by the ship captain — Pascal — a cousin of Stéphanie's. Robbie surreptitiously brushed the shiny wheel while the men tried to translate the French words on the various control indicators. The cruise had only started when Pascal announced that Lieutenant Commander Dave was to step in as helmsman, "until he

saw the Statue of Liberty." After some hesitation, Dave complied,
guessing that he was not meant to take the cruise boat all the
way to New York harbour. Obviously, some riddle was to be
expected at a bachelor's party. The Eiffel Tower slowly shrunk
on the port side and stern, and still no Statue of Liberty. The
Edith Piaf was heading farther downstream when Dave tri-
umphantly uttered "Target in sight", pointing his finger at the
control screen of the boat's rear camera. Captain Pascal congratulated him and stepped back at the steering wheel. After an
impressive u-turn, the large vessel started upstream, towards a
twelve-meter-high replica of the Ellis Island statue. "A gift from
your country," Pascal commented. Having passed his unofficial
test as *bateau-mouche* captain, Lieutenant Commander Dave
was allowed to sit with his friends for a festive dinner on the
panoramic bridge.

Their group naturally attracted the attention of their fellow passengers. Not often does one come across five youngish
Service Dress White uniformed U. S. Coast Guard officers on
the Seine. Robbie's fingers spontaneously came up to feel the
chaplain's badge on his chest, as he tried to ignore the friendly
smiles of half a dozen elegant young Spanish-speaking women
at a nearby table, who seemed to be part of a bachelorette party.
One of them wearing blue had a particularly fine face, with eyes
rather similar, he remembered, to that of an actress he'd liked
(unless it was her nose?). One of them, perhaps, would get
married the following day, like Dave. Was then another woman
among them, perhaps, a nun in civvies, as he was a priest in
disguise? Repressed giggles interrupted Robbie's thoughts as he
understood that the bride-to-be had asked her retinue whether
the five officers were part of the entertainment for her party.
Robbie felt ill at ease. He should make his consecration to God
clear. Standing up, he blessed the first dishes while his friends,
taken by surprise, signed themselves hesitantly (all but Sam,
who was Jewish). Silence followed around the neighbouring

tables. Now, his status was clearly manifested and any ambiguity was removed. A glass of champagne did away with Robbie's unease and the various conversations were resumed in a slightly subdued tone as the lit towers of Notre-Dame grew larger ahead of them, in the hot and humid evening breeze.

The five men exchanged fond memories and cracked many a joke. Dave looked incredulous when unwrapping a framed picture of them as teenagers, handed him by Pete. A seventeen-year-old Dave was depicted sitting in a rusted van, holding some political pamphlet entitled *The Ottaviani Intervention.* More striking than the pipe in Dave's mouth was his peculiar red t-shirt. It bore a black Templar knight with one knee down and his hands resting on the hilt of a long sword, with the rather anachronistic motto "*No weed; no gals.*" Below this little medieval warning spread a cryptic invitation: "*Stuck for the Old Mass? Call L. I. S.! Deployment within the hour guaranteed.*" As Dave and Pete burst into laughter, Mike enlightened Sam and Robbie.

"*L. I. S.* stood for *Liturgical Intervention Squad,* which we founded in 1988. Anyone across the state needing a traditional Latin Mass could call us and we would bring literally every item, from chalice and reliquaries, to maniples and incense spoon; even a tent and carpets if they had no church. We only asked them to provide the priest. We organised dozens of funeral Masses, and even some weddings. We gradually gave up though when entering Cape May." Dave begged them not to bring their horrendous red t-shirts, in case the *L. I. S.* should be secretly resurrected for his own wedding the following morning. Robbie knew that his three friends were practising Catholics, but he was a bit hurt to find out only then how much more committed they had been than he had guessed during their Coast Guard years. As he smiled cheerfully, he felt slightly left out, not having been admitted to share their secret sooner, when out of their group *he* was the one who had become a priest

and when, unlike Sam who was Jewish, he would have taken
an interest in their teenage feats.

The *Edith Piaf* was now moored along *Ile Saint-Louis*, with
Notre-Dame in the distance. Around 11pm, romantic music
played and a few couples started dancing. Sam asked one of the
young Spanish-speaking ladies at the manless table for a dance,
an offer readily accepted and successfully reiterated by Pete and
even Mike. Still seated, Robbie smiled at Dave with a hint of
embarrassment as both noticed the three remaining women's
likely expectation. The one in the blue dress, though, was gazing
at the nearby cathedral. Regardless, he would not budge. He
belonged to Christ exclusively, and Dave to his bride. Back at
the table, Mike announced that the bachelor party would soon
rise to its climax with an exclusive cabaret show near Montmartre. Robbie knew that impropriety was unlikely with such
men as Dave and Mike. But he still felt relieved to be excused
from the entertainment, thanks to his priestly status.

Alighting before midnight, he stepped upon the cobbled quay
again in happy dizziness. His fingers seemed to remember the
soft contact of the wooden wheel on the navigation bridge, and
he treasured the sensation of having almost steered the vessel,
as if in charge of the six-hundred passengers — even if only for
three seconds. "Six hundred souls, that's about the size of our
Sunday congregation, back in Philly," he reckoned. He distractedly returned the "Buenas noches" of the six Spanish-speaking
girls as they entered a pink limo awaiting them by the ship.
He followed the ramp up towards Place de la Concorde. The
air was moist and still very hot under the dark clouds as he
walked leisurely towards the ancient obelisk in the centre of
the great square. He lit a cigarette and remained standing, his
hands in his pockets and his white cap on. In the distance, a
few fireworks could be seen, in anticipation of the national
celebration the following day. The breeze carried refreshing
droplets from the large fountains skirted by a sheet of water

flowing evenly from the rim of the basin like a huge shell or flower. He would have liked to dive into the cool water and simply sit there, looking at the sky.

While Robbie stood relishing the unique beauty of the site, a large pink fancy car parked along the pavement: "Excuse me, Officer, can I speak with you?" Robbie recognised the Spanish-speaking bachelorette party. One of the young women stepped out and the car drove off. He was perplexed and slightly worried when recognising her blue dress.

"Hi. I'm a Catholic girl from Mexico. My friends will pick me up again in five minutes. I meant to ask you, while on the boat... Are you a soldier, or a Catholic priest?"

"Good evening. I was a U. S. Coast Guard for a few years. But now I am a priest, you're correct. I'm a curate on the East Coast of the U. S."

"Then you must know why we Mexicans visit the Shrine of Our Lady of Guadalupe?"

Wondering whether she was testing him, Robbie replied: "Not only Mexicans travel there, I think. I went once on a pilgrimage and venerated the *tilma* of Blessed Juan Diego. I keep a copy of the Virgin's image in my breviary" (which he'd left at the flat with his daily prayers unfinished before midnight, he guiltily realised). The young woman seemed relieved and finally asked: "If you are a Roman Catholic priest, can you hear my confession now, here in Paris?"

Robbie was taken aback. He had been prepared for many things, but not for such a request. And how could he answer it in the middle of this vast square, with no churches around, or none open, surely? On the other hand, the young woman might be sincere and truly in need of his ministry. She looked a bit weary, rather than mischievous. Realising that he had not taken his stole with him, he quickly checked what the options were. He could simply bless her and noncommittally walk away. He could also invite her to the Lemberts' flat across the square, where his stole was—and . . . no, this was out of the question!

"Listen, I can hear your confession here and now, if you wish—but I don't have a stole with me."

As she agreed, he turned toward *Rue Royale* and pointed at the façade of *Sainte Madeleine* Church, "where the Lord Jesus dwells," suggesting that she prayed a little in preparation for the sacrament. Robbie heard the woman and gave his first absolution in Europe. "And I absolve you from all your sins, in the name of the Father, and of the Son, and of the Holy Spirit." When was the last time a priest had uttered these words in the middle of that famous square, he wondered. He had a faint remembrance that it might have been during the French Revolution, as Catholics had been executed on that very spot.

Walking home after the fancy car had fetched his mysterious penitent, the young priest gave thanks for the grace of his ministry. It started raining and he reached the porch of the flat just in time.

*   *   *

With a gloomy look on his face that Saturday morning, Robbie had just finished shaving. Against his expectations, Bastille Day was not looking good. He had woken up in a bad mood for three reasons. First, he felt exhausted, having been unable to fall asleep until after 3:00am (if it was not jetlag, it must have been the champagne). Second, the sound of heavy rain against the shutters of his window confirmed the alarming forecast for the military parade (and for the wedding reception). Third, his phone displayed a text message from his mother. That truly was the last straw. As he was leaving the day before, his mum had suggested that he might try to locate and visit the religious community where her own mother had stayed during the War: "Have a picture of you taken there if you can—Granddad might like it!" she had added. She had now texted him the exact address, *Couvent Sainte Claire, 8bis Rue des Repenties, 75009 Paris*. Robbie's grandmother had passed away years before his birth. He had only heard her mentioned as the affectionate "Granny." He vaguely recalled that, a refugee from Silesia, Alma Kravitz had been given shelter by French nuns in Paris before making her way to America in 1945 with a young U. S. Marine, his own grandfather, whose present Alzheimer's still allowed occasional spells of awareness. Well, there was nothing extraordinary there: many Americans have European origins, don't they? But when on earth would he find the time to visit this unknown place? That was the issue. This Saturday afternoon would be busy with the wedding reception, and convents would surely not receive visitors in the evening. He was leaving the following morning for Lourdes with an American pilgrimage, including his comrades from the Coast Guards Pete and even Sam (merely a Jewish sightseer in this instance, not a pilgrim), plus two fellow priests from Philly attending with their parishioners. His ticket from Paris-Austerlitz railway station had been purchased long ago. Thus, he would text his mother that the convent-hunting would have to wait for another occasion. Unless of course, instead of . . . Yes, it *could* work. What could? That was precisely what upset Robbie as he dropped his phone on the spare pillow, while against his shutters the rain sounded even louder.

"The French breakfast for you with *croissants*, Father Robbie, that is ready at the moment!" The young man welcomed the Portuguese housekeeper's knock at his door as a diversion from the infuriating thought that had just crossed his mind: that of finding his grandmother's convent right after his Mass *instead* of watching the launch of the military parade. Yes, that would be a worthy sacrifice. Sitting by himself in the dining room, he tried to drown his anger in his coffee cup. "Sacrifice?" Why always sacrifice—he was on holiday and in *Paris* of all places! Was it not enough to sacrifice most of the parade so as to arrive on time at that much-too-early wedding? Was he now to give up even that tantalising sample of the Bastille Day show, for the vague hope of locating a pre-WWII convent, which probably had been turned into a hotel or a fitness club by now? And for what, anyway? To have a picture of him taken for his demential Granddad who, most likely, would have no clue as to why his daughter would put it under his nose with an insistent smile?

Checking his watch, he stopped eating to keep the one-hour Eucharistic fast, realising that he should soon get on his way to *Sainte Madeleine* Church. For a moment, he wished he hadn't brought along his Coast Guard uniform. How tempting to put it on there and then (one very last time) and mingle with the foreign regiments waiting to take part in the military parade! At that instant outside the Élysée Palace, possibly, one hundred Republican Guards were saddling their horses, while at Le Bourget air base, Dassault *Rafale* fighters from the French Air Force were surely rehearsing the demonstration flight soon to be performed above the Champ-Élysées. Was he to miss all of it? Back in his room, he felt the smooth surface of the brass USCG Ensign lapel pin flag he meant to wear on his clerical suit at the wedding, after he had worn his Chaplain pin on his Coast Guard uniform the evening before. Was Ensign Edgworth truly gone—Fr Robbie?

His eyes caught sight of another item packed in his large suitcase. It was a compact portable Mass kit in a metal case, similar to the one used by U. S. padres during WWII. In fact, a film about Fr Francis Sampson, a regimental chaplain for the 501st Parachute Infantry Regiment of the 101st Airborne Division, had struck a chord with him when he was still a Coast Guard. It might have been what steered him towards the priesthood, who could tell? Robbie recalled the famous scene when Fr Samson parachuted into a river in Normandy on D-Day, and had to dive several times to retrieve his Mass kit from the murky waters. Speaking of water, in his turn he would soon have to dive into that downpour on his way to church, although not under enemy fire. Would he wear his uniform? His *priestly* uniform? Yes he would! Let them try and deter him, Robbie mumbled, while buttoning his black polyester cassock. That was settled. He grabbed in one hand the old leather handle of the metal case, caught his small foldable umbrella in the other hand, and resolutely walked down to the entrance hall of the building. He was a priest. God had to be glorified. Souls were to be saved. He would offer Mass and everything would fall into place.

Upon reaching the street, Robbie was disconcerted by the heaviness of the rain. His small umbrella provided a totally insufficient protection against the summer torrents falling from the Parisian sky. He ignored the idea of walking back to the flat to ask Elvira for a larger umbrella. Out of the question! There would be no retreat, and no surrender either (please God). He gave thanks for the reconnaissance with Mr Lembert the afternoon before, which allowed him to dart straight to *Sainte Madeleine* Church. Climbing two steps at a time the high stairs before the neo-classical façade, he rushed for shelter under the vast colonnade outside the church and, making his way inside, came face to face with Napoleon! The French Emperor was displayed in full regalia on a large fresco above the high altar, entering heaven, no less. It was a bit too much for Robbie's taste, even for the glorious embodiment of the self-made man. The young priest had a more urgent matter to attend to, however. Robbie walked down the aisle across the empty nave and, having genuflected before the tabernacle, knocked at a side door bearing a *Sacristy* sign. After several minutes and one more knock, a tired-looking layman let him in. Producing his *celebret* from Philadelphia, Robbie explained that he had booked a slot with Mr Lembert for his Mass at 8.30am. The sacristan checked the name on the register and, without further inquiry, led Robbie down a narrow staircase into the crypt. Having gestured his gratitude for being allowed to offer Mass on that altar, he started unpacking his items while the sacristan went to fetch water and wine.

On his return, the man looked suspiciously at Robbie, as if only then noticing his wet cassock. As he set the cruets on the altar, he realised that Robbie had turned the missal stand and crucifix to say Mass facing the tabernacle rather than toward the empty crypt. This seemed to upset the sacristan, who bluntly turned back the items in their original position. Meanwhile, Robbie was taking out of his suitcase his compact Latin travel altar missal. The sacristan pointed at the cover, saying that he had to use the French missal provided, or the English one allocated to foreign priests visiting, since "integrist Masses were not permitted in that church." Robbie showed him that his missal was the Novus Ordo Latin one, actually the Jubilee Edition printed the year before, in 2000. Things got worse when, assuming he had reassured the sacristan, Robbie started turning the missal stand again to face the tabernacle. No water this time, but strong protests, were showered upon the bewildered priest who managed to identify the words "the Second Vatican Council," "Catholic," and "integrist" occurring several times. It was by then past 8.45am and Robbie was becoming aware of having to move on. Politely, but firmly, he explained—in English though—that it was absolutely fine to offer Mass the way he meant, pointing on the page at the rubric "*ad populum conversus*," that is, "*the priest having turned around toward the people*," which implies that his standard posture is facing the tabernacle rather than the nave.

By then the sacristan looked convinced that Robbie was some sort of heretic. He stood between the altar and the priest as if to prevent sacrilege, warning that he "would wait for Monseigneur André" (probably the pastor), "who would arrive for the 9.30am Mass and who would tell him in person what was allowed at *Sainte Madeleine* and what was not, since one was not in Rome or in America but in Paris." Robbie could not believe such an unfair reaction. The sacristan could not ignore that his priestly superior had himself entered Robbie's name into the Mass register the afternoon before, at the request of his well-known parishioner Mr Lembert. There was no way he would wait nearly an hour to learn if the parish priest would eventually let him offer Mass. On the other hand, for the sake of expediency, should he not comply and say Mass turning his back on God? But why should he! His pastor didn't object to his facing East, back at Philly. Here the nave was still empty and facing the tabernacle was his strict right. How did that layman dare prevent him, a priest in perfect good standing, from fulfilling an essential part of his ministry? Rather than letting anger take hold of him, he waited in silence for a little while, trying to pray to God in the tabernacle (hidden behind the sacristan). His opponent showing every intention not to negotiate, Robbie noisily packed his items, genuflected and left.

He should find another church as soon as possible. Standing under the church colonnade before diving again into the heavy rain, Robbie unfolded the tourist map he had been given in the airport shuttle and spotted St Augustine Church straight to his right. Walking along "*Boulevard Malesherbes*" took longer than it looked on paper and by then, the soaked cassock stuck along the legs of the priest, shortening his strides. The pavement was empty and very few cars drove by. Parisians were still in bed (understandably on a Saturday before 9am), or away in the country for the bank holiday. Through the downpour, Robbie nearly bumped into a knight in greenish armour, on horseback. It was no Republican Guard on his way to the parade but, as it appeared, a bronze sculpture of St Joan of Arc. "Help me offer Mass here, I beg you St Joan!" Robbie asked the saint as he reached the church railing. Dropping his metal suitcase while keeping his small umbrella in his other hand for theoretical protection, the priest shook in vain the closed gate. "Unbelievable, it is locked! Do no French pray on Bastille Day?" With growing concern, Robbie rushed along the building, hoping for some side entrance, only to find a sign announcing closure for

maintenance until the 6.30pm Sunday Vigil Mass. His heart
sank at this new failure. Suddenly becoming aware of a wet
sensation around his toes, and heels, he realised that water
actually ran inside his shoes by then, as if he were wearing
flip-flops by the beach, with ripples up to his ankles.

At that stage, his mood combined exasperation, humour and
determination. With no shelter in sight, he managed to unfold
his map again under the tiny umbrella. The wet paper was now
close to melting. Churches were not displayed as significant
attractions, but fairly close to his location was the *"Galeries
Lafayette,"* an upmarket department store. Was it a sign? Well,
since St Joan of Arc had let him down (apparently thinking
him some English foe), General Lafayette might well come
to his rescue (although not a saint, he'd helped Americans
before, hadn't he?). Robbie waved at a cab passing him in
splashing water, but the driver clearly preferred not to allow
his unidentified wet dark shape into his cosy (and dry) car.
Not knowing where the few buses in sight were heading to, he
could only keep walking along *"Boulevard Haussmann."* The old
leather handle of his vintage WII case felt increasingly weak
in his hand and the priest expected it to break any time. He
should urgently find a church, or he would need to go home
and change all his clothes. After about five minutes, as the
"Galeries Lafayette" appeared on his left, his plea was heard
when a sign materialised, bearing the words "Catholic Church."
Robbie ran toward its porch in a side street and pushed the
mercifully unlocked door. Panting, he genuflected by the tabernacle, keeping his suitcase on the kneeler safe from the pool
spreading from his drenched apparel across the marble tiles.
The Crown of Thorns in his hands, King St Louis, no less, was
looking at him from his niche in the sanctuary. As Robbie
surveyed the church in search for available altars, he happily
counted at least seven. Thus, there would be no problem for
him to offer Mass at last.

It was only quarter past nine. His eyes met the *Confession* sign and he thought it a good opportunity to recollect before Mass. It did not take him long to examine his conscience, as he was a frequent penitent, confessing several times a year. Thankfully the other priest understood English. On his way out of the confessional, Robbie enquired with the priest whether he could offer his Mass at one of the many altars. An inviting smile on his face, his colleague replied that he was most welcome to concelebrate the next scheduled Mass with him and his curate at five past twelve, "after the Angelus." Robbie assumed that he was talking to the pastor and replied that he could sadly not wait until midday, being on his way to preach at a wedding planned for 11am. As the French priest enquired about concelebrating the wedding Mass, Robbie had to explain that it was not possible in the traditional Latin rite. The smile on the cleric's face seemed to become more intense as he suggested Robbie might then come back and concelebrate the 6pm Sunday vigil Mass later that afternoon, if he wished. Robbie was beginning to feel upset. Why these long negotiations when all altars were available immediately? He finally summed up the situation:

"Father, I am a very soaked American priest from the Archdiocese of Philadelphia. Here is my *celebret*. I have tried in vain two other churches and it's still pouring with rain outside. I should really offer Mass now. I have all I need in my suitcase and I know your penitents want you. So, may I ask your sacristan for a free altar now?" Robbie would never forget the answer. It was a remarkably concise one, uttered with a fraternal smile and supported by a deep, penetrating green gaze: "No."

* * *

The microwave would not do, as they had metal bits in them, Robbie decided, laying his drenched shoes inside the electric oven instead. "Served with Dijon mustard, Monsieur, or plain thyme?" — Robbie asked within himself in an unlikely

impersonation of a French waiter. Drying his more formal foot-
wear was an emergency since he could not really attend the wedding wearing his Nike trainers. By the time he had walked back
to the flat it was now close to 10am and all his fancy plans were
sunk of course: whether the military parade, his mum's convent
hunting, or even his private Mass. Robbie would consider himself lucky enough if he could arrive on time — and reasonably
dry — to deliver his wedding homily. Standing barefoot in shorts
and t-shirt before the oven, he was glad that the need to act
promptly prevented him from thinking at leisure about what had
just occurred. And yet, had that French priest really just denied
him access to an altar? He checked again the list of sins he had
confessed to him prior to their conversation. No, he knew well
that not one of them justified this incredible sanction. If anything, Robbie impartially reckoned, his confession should rather
have shown him a dutiful young priest with a sincere desire to
serve God and souls. How on earth then could this priest at an
important Parisian parish have turned him away! Did he doubt
his priesthood? But he had not even looked at his *celebret*. Had
perhaps the sacristan at *Sainte Madeleine* rang all neighbouring
churches to warn against a sacrilegious American priest?

He took his cassock out of the drier. It looked less like a mop,
but another twenty minutes would have been necessary to dry
it fully. Barely half an hour from then however, Robbie would
need to be in church to welcome the bridal couple and to deliver
his homily soon after.

Sitting in the taxi ordered for him by Elvira, his Mass kit
on the seat next to him just in case, with one hand he hastily
painted his discoloured cooked shoes with black polish, while
rehearsing the typed sermon he held in his other hand. What
if *these* sheets of paper had been in his soaked pockets earlier
that morning: they would have disintegrated and he should have
had to improvise. Arrived at *Rue Sainte Claire*, he did not wait
for the change from the cabby and instead, trying to hide his

wet cassock under his dry surplice, he rushed into *Sainte Claire* Chapel where all guests, the bridegroom and the priest celebrant were already waiting. Robbie and Dave smiled in mutual relief. Thank God, he had made it on time!

After the wedding, the reception conveniently took place in a hall within the same block (the other side of the building was a care home). There would be no risk of getting wet again, although the clouds looked lighter through the windows and the rain now fell thinly across the patio and garden. Robbie did not dare and try yet a fourth time to ask for permission to offer Mass that day. Clearly, it was not to happen. Lunch was to follow the refreshments, a bit later. Feeling no hunger but dire thirst despite his immersion in water that morning, he sat at random among the guests, a glass of *Perrier* in hand. Captain Pascal, of the *Edith Piaf* bateau-mouche, asked him if he was pleased with his first stay in Paris so far. Robbie preferred to skip the painful episode in the morning and warmly praised the cruise on the Seine the night before. Pascal knew that he was staying at the Lemberts'. Robbie assured him that he regretted not having had the opportunity to chat further with his generous host, a kind retired gentleman, who had had to go away to the country. Was Mr Lembert by any chance Belgian or Swiss rather than French, Robbie inquired, since he seemed somehow unconcerned to have to miss the Bastille Day celebrations? Pascal laughed frankly and, to the amazement of Robbie, gave a description of the unassuming old man which seemed to refer to someone totally different.

"Too bad he had to miss the wedding of his friends' daughter. Every year on 14th July, he leads the festivities in his wife's home village where he is the mayor, in the West Country."

"Really? I did not expect him to be such a patriot."

"His wife's ancestor Jacques Cathelineau died this very day, 208 years ago I believe. He was the Generalissimo of the Catholic and Royal Army against the Republicans during the Vendée Wars."

"You mean, he was an aristocrat?"

"Rather the opposite. Cathelineau was a mere peddler, selling goods from village to village. But his reputation as a saint led to his being chosen as leader. The aristocrat generals, as you call them, obeyed the peddler's orders. Over there in the Vendée, as we speak, they're having a procession in honour of the martyrs killed by the Revolutionaries, followed by fireworks by sunset."

"So, on 14th July, not all French people celebrate Bastille Day?"

"Many of us would rather commemorate the liberation of Jerusalem by the Crusaders, which occurred in the night of 14th July 1099."

"What! Really? I had never imagined this. But what about Mr Lembert then? If he honours a Counter-Revolutionary leader and yet is the village mayor, how can he be loyal to the Republic?"

"Really Father, don't tell me nobody explained to you in whose flat you are staying! I assumed that as a former Navy officer you would have been told about 'Major Guy.' Guy Lembert, Viscount de Villefronde, was one of the few French officers who managed to escape Colditz (the German fortress, I mean, not the video game) during WWII. He made his way from North East Germany to France, walking by night in freezing snow while being hunted by the Nazis. Back in France, he coordinated the *Vélite-Thermopyles* Resistance network in Lyon and the surrounding area, saving hundreds of refugees, including about 45 Jews. Even though he's not a great Bastille supporter, you may call him a patriot."

Sam joined the conversation, wondering how every Frenchman seemed to have been in the Resistance during WWII. Pascal wittily admitted that genuine French *résistants* were surely far fewer than the Americans claiming to have had an ancestor on the *Mayflower*.

"Touché!" said Sam.

"I'm not a *Mayflower* descendant," Robbie ventured. "My people came from Ireland later in the early 1900s. My granddad even visited there every few years later on. As a child, I was always fascinated by the trophy kept on the wall in his study: a glazed frame with a huge taxidermy trout mount, looking harmless enough above the brass inscription *Firmount Angling Society, Largest Catch, by Eamonn Edgeworth, of Philadelphia, 1971.*"

"Speaking of fish, look at the menu: we will start with *terrine de saumon fumé au fromage frais.* Let us make our way to the tables," Pascal suggested.

The clouds had practically cleared and, after a five-course lunch in the garden, various wines and a lot of talking, Robbie felt the need for quiet and went back to the chapel. There, he was surprised to see Sam, sitting with his eyes shut. Robbie knelt down further to the side. He thanked God for the gift of his priesthood and resolved to forgive with all his heart the sacristan and the priest who had prevented him from offering Mass that morning. Forgiveness though was more easily decided in his mind than felt in his heart, he realised. After about twenty minutes, his slumberous meditation was interrupted when two aged sisters from the care home wheeled in an even older female patient, followed by other elderly residents who sat in the pews close to the Lady statue. One sister said in a loud voice to the white-haired woman in the wheelchair: "As usual the first decade is for you, Sister Paulette." The old patient did not reply, but a faint smile flashed across her wrinkled face.

At the end of the five decades, prayed in French, Robbie unexpectedly felt confident enough to try yet a fourth time to offer Mass. In the sacristy, he introduced himself to a middle-aged sister who looked at his diocesan *celebret*. On her answering that they had no English missal to lend him but only a traditional Latin one, Robbie assumed that his attempt would be unsuccessful once again. He extracted from his suitcase his new Latin missal, thankfully dry under its plastic wrapping. Still slightly incredulous, he saw the sister set the cruets and lit the candles on the altar against the wall, facing the tabernacle. She asked if he could wait until she found an altar server, Sam having understandably declined her request. But Robbie was anxious to begin as soon as possible, lest another obstacle would ruin his last chance of offering Mass. Proceeding to the altar, he eventually managed to offer the holy Sacrifice, praying among others for the senile sister on her wheelchair and for his grandfather.

* * *

Robbie never got a chance to visit France again since that first stay, and his mother understood well that her request could not be met in the short time her son had spent in Paris. Some twelve years later, on the tenth anniversary of his conversion to Catholicism, Sam made his solemn profession as a Benedictine monk at a new monastery in the Ozark foothills of Oklahoma. Robbie and he walked in the garden that afternoon, Sam recalling the twists and turns in his spiritual journey, from Jewish Coast Guard officer to Catholic monk. Robbie was no longer a junior priest by then and had listened to many sad and happy confidences. Still, he felt his heartbeat accelerate slightly when Sam, now Brother Paulinus, referred to an old bed-ridden nun as a "Righteous Among the Nations" who had hidden in her Paris convent half a dozen Jewish girls from Eastern Europe during WWII. Sam had only met that nun twice after Dave's wedding, but he credited her with his conversion.

The Wi-Fi connection in the abbey guesthouse was acceptable. It took Robbie twenty seconds (if one discounts the twelve years elapsed) to verify that in the 9th arrondissement of Paris, at the foot of Montmartre, *Rue Sainte Claire* runs parallel to *Rue des Repenties*, on either side of a care home until recently staffed by nuns, formerly a convent of Poor Clares. Sam was right: the only personality connected with the place was one Sister Paulette, long passed away, who had offered shelter to Jewish refugees in the 1940s. Halfway down the list of those saved, the hyperlink on the name of Alma Kravitz was faulty, leading nowhere apparently. Hearing the bells ringing for Vespers at the abbey church, Robbie shut his laptop and made his way to prayer, smiling at the last piece of information learnt from the Wikipedia page of *Sainte Claire* Convent, whose "19th century neo-gothic chapel of rather poor architectural merit can be accessed from either street."

V

The Roofs of Africa
(2015, TANZANIA)

NOTHER GLASS OF ORANGE JUICE
wouldn't go amiss, Fr Isidore decided, seated at a
table in the shade with his back against the wall. The
terrace outside the dining room at Honey Badger Lodge was
nearly empty. Most other guests were in town or on their way
back from the mountain, while his small team were checking the equipment for the climb on the following morning.
Although the short flight from Kigali had been a bit bumpy,
he knew that his liturgical items were securely packed in his
Mass kit case, including the precious Mass wine. He had not
wished to look at the Kilimanjaro from the plane, feeling
that it would be a lack of respect for the giant volcano, the
fourth most prominent point on Earth. But now that he was
in Moshi, he was seeing it in the distance, the great snow-
capped mountain. To think that in five days, please God, he
would be offering Mass at Uhuru Peak, the highest point in
Africa at 5,895 metres above sea level. It would be so quiet, up
there ... Actually, even here at the Lodge, little could be heard:
a few birds, some vehicles parking, and perhaps a mosquito.
Feeling like dozing a bit in his chair, he tightened his light
scarf around his Roman collar against any insects. The stillness
ended abruptly though, when a large group of men irrupted,
singing and clasping each other. A couple of women accompanied them. All had just come down from the Kilimanjaro
and seemed in the best of moods to celebrate their successful
ascent to the roof of Africa. They hastily opened cans of chilled
beer produced by a waiter, while throwing a rugby ball over
the head of Fr Isidore (not knowing him to be a priest, surely)
and shouting for excitement.

Fr Isidore smiled at their rowdiness. Now in his mid fifties, "Fr Easy" (he liked this pun on the first two syllables of his name) had travelled extensively even outside Africa and had come across all sorts of human types, some far rougher than these Englishmen — starting with his own Rwandan people. Besides, he found the coincidence amusing, having been a rugby coach in Kigali long before the Silverbacks would become the national rugby team in 2003. Meanwhile, the 1994 civil war had taken all that he cherished most, until God called him to His service as a priest. These players who had just arrived, were they League or Union, he wondered. One of them, of Indian descent, let himself fall on the chair next to him, laughing and drinking his second or perhaps third beer. Fr Isidore's attention was caught by the man's tattoo. The rolled up sleeve of his sports shirt revealed above the wrist a blazing sun bearing an acronym in Gothic font in its centre, with no nails depicted below, though. As the trend for tattoos spread, mystical and cryptic patterns were becoming popular. Still, Fr Isidore wondered if it was a good idea for this youngish-looking lad to wear on his skin the emblem of the most renowned priestly order in the Catholic Church, as if it were the name of a heavy metal band.

Pouring more juice into his glass, the priest engaged him in conversation.

"So, which route did you take?"

"The Marangu one, like most people apparently. We all made it to Uhuru Peak, despite carrying a lot of extra stuff. We even brought inflatable posts. In addition, I had my filming equipment."

"Are you a film crew then, or some kind of Olympic team?"

"We're amateur rugby players, but we've just made history though!"

"Don't tell me you played rugby on that mountain?"

"Sure we did! I mean, my mates did, while I filmed their feat. We'd informed the Guinness Book of Records guys and made sure we had every proof to justify the new entry. Imagine that, man: 'Warburton Team becomes first to play a full rugby league game on the roof of Africa.' Altitude sickness was a major issue for most of the team as their bodies were pushed to the limit physically and mentally. Climbing Kilimanjaro in six days is a tough task alone, you must know, but when you combine this with a full rugby match at high altitude, then stamina, fitness and mental determination are tested to the max."

Genuinely impressed as he was, Fr Isidore had nearly forgotten to enquire about the man's tattoo. Pointing at it, he then ventured: "This picture on your arm, it's not the Warburton Rugby Club logo, is it?" The young man was interrupted by the ball playfully thrown his way, which he managed to catch without spilling his beer. His reply, given with light-hearted indifference, took Fr Isidore aback:

"That? It's a Christian society. 'Jesuits,' they're called. I'm on leave from them. Are you a believer?"

Fr Isidore became intrigued. Could this young fellow be a Jesuit? Had he left the priesthood? Realising that his interlocutor took him for a layman, he loosened his scarf, revealing his Roman collar while stating, loudly enough to be heard in spite of the shouting rugbymen:

"I do believe that Jesus is God. However I'm just a parish priest in Rwanda, not a Jesuit. I'm Easy by the way, Fr Easy, on my way to the big mountain."

With a look of surprise, the young man replied as loudly: "Wow! I hadn't thought priests climbed mountains. Also, you look old enough to be my father. Won't it be a bit tough for you, if you don't mind my asking? There's little oxygen up there, you know? Unless you take the Lemosho Route, giving two more days to acclimatise."

"Don't you worry, my friend. I need just enough oxygen for my altar candles to burn. I'm going to offer Mass on that summit. For years I've been wanting to bless Africa with the Host and now it's about to happen."

The young man sipped his beer, not commenting. Most members of his group were leaving the terrace, proclaiming that they would now enjoy the longest shower in their lives.

Fr Isidore expected the young fellow to imitate them soon. But he seemed in no hurry to shed the dust and sweat of the ascent. Instead, he reclined in his seat, gazing towards distant Kilimanjaro. Quiet had returned across the terrace, with just a few birds tweeting. After five minutes in silence, the priest ventured: "What's your name anyway?"

"I'm just Sammy—not *Father* Sammy, since I left the Jesuits while still a student."

"A student, hey? What was your field of study?"

"I graduated in film direction two years ago, in 2013. I love it."

"Filming? That's funny. I thought Jesuits were focused on high theology: De Lubac, Hans Küng, Rahner, that kind of stuff."

"Of course—although Küng isn't a Jesuit. I started a doctoral thesis on Teilhard de Chardin, a French palaeontologist priest—also a Jesuit. But this is all behind me now. Even if I wanted to complete my thesis, I probably could not, as Heythrop announced they would shut down soon. Heythrop College is where I studied, in London. You know what?—Teilhard would have loved climbing Kilimanjaro, since he grew up on a volcano."

"Teilhard de Chardin . . . I've heard his name before. Remind me, was he not the one who said that Christ and the material world were converging, and eventually would be recognised as one and the same thing?"

"Pretty much so, yes. It'll be the completion of history, the Omega Point. My word, Father, for one in parish ministry, you are super well-read."

"Not extensively. But in Germany where I trained for the priesthood, they told us a few things about Teilhard and others. Theology wasn't my first love, though. My turn to impress you: you wouldn't guess what I was before entering seminary: a rugby coach, in Kigali."

"You—a rugby coach! You're kidding me, Fr Easy! I wish you had been with us yesterday for the game at Uhuru Peak. That would've been amazing. Want a beer? It's on our team. From rugbymen to a rugbyman."

"Not now, thanks, but on my way down in six days, please God, sure. I'll drink one to your good health. Now, goodbye Sammy, and God bless. I must pray Compline before going to bed. I'll have an early rise tomorrow—while you'll enjoy a well-deserved lie-in."

As Fr Isidore stood up from behind the table, Sammy realised that the priest was actually wearing a cassock. The sight of the black silhouette struck something buried deep in the young man's heart. Now feeling weary, he found it wiser to drag himself into his room and take his long-awaited shower, for fear of collapsing into deep slumber there and then on the terrace.

* * *

A bed. A real bed with a mattress and sheets and four pillows all to himself. And yet, Sammy could not sleep. The celebratory dinner that evening had been memorable. Where did they find such wine in a place like Moshi? Probably imported from South Africa. The guys were in surprisingly great shape despite their exhaustion. Harry's post on Facebook had already gone viral: "World record, mates! Rugby game on the roof of Africa—at 19341ft! Our 38 strong team split into two groups and played for a full 80 minutes. After a lot of wheezing and long drink breaks, the score finished 10-10. In so much pain it's unreal. So glad to be down the mountain now. We're in bits. Never ever again. So proud of all the team's achievements! We've been thru hell and back!"

After dinner, Sammy had shot a video of the team surrounding Sue, lovelier than ever in her Tanzanian green kanga dress (the colour of fertility, someone had commented), while she held her giant £162,337 cheque. Such was the impressive amount

raised for the Steve Driscoll Charity for disabled athletes. Sue
Driscoll and some colleagues had set it up in memory of her
late husband, a professional rugby player who had died of
bowel cancer. Teasers of Sammy's films of the ascent and of
the game were now online, with added comments from the
referee. Sammy was not surprised that Sue had made it to the
summit. Although a widow, she was barely thirty and very fit.
In truth, what an amazing woman she was. Briefly hugging him,
she said she loved his video at Uhuru Peak, immortalizing the
team's victory: "They ran, but *you* made their efforts visible to
the whole world." Well, if *that* wasn't a sign ... He would need
to speak up to her soon: this very night, in fact.

Standing outside his hut, Sammy looked with delight at the
snow-covered tip of Mount Kilimanjaro, reflecting the moon-
light. "There are teams up there," he reckoned, "about to wake
up and make it to the summit, like us yesterday." It was Sammy's first opportunity to analyse what he had felt while on the
mountain. His experience could best be expressed, he thought,
through the words of Teilhard de Chardin: "*Remain true to
yourself, but move ever upward toward greater consciousness and
greater love! At the summit you will find yourselves united with
all those who, from every direction, have made the same ascent.
For everything that rises must converge.*" Yes, the companionship
within the team and with nature over the past six days was
the closest confirmation he'd ever encountered of Teilhard's
prophetic intuition. He knew by heart the celebrated opening
of *Mass upon the World*, recalling the occasion when, in 1923,
the Jesuit priest had found himself on a scientific expedition
in Mongolia with no host and wine to offer Mass:

"*Since once again, Lord ... I have neither bread, nor wine, nor
altar, I will raise myself beyond these symbols, up to the pure
majesty of the real itself; I, your priest, will make the whole world
my altar and on it will offer you all the labours and sufferings of
the world. Over there, on the horizon, the sun has just touched*

with light the outermost fringe of the eastern sky. Once again,
beneath this moving sheet of fire, the living surface of the earth
wakes and, once again, begins its fearful travail."

Sammy had used that text many times as part of a liturgical
Offertory experiment with fellow students. This was the moment
when bread and wine were brought to the lay person presiding:

"I will place on my paten, O God, the harvest to be won by
this renewal of labour. Into my chalice I shall pour all the sap
which is to be pressed out this day from the earth's fruits. My
chalice and my paten are the depths of a soul laid widely open
to all the forces which in a moment will rise up from every
corner of the earth and converge upon the Spirit. Grant me the
remembrance and the mystic presence of all those whom the light
is now awakening to a new day."

Yes, that was what he'd felt at Uhuru Peak, at dawn. Admittedly, he was not a priest in a sacramental sense, but he was so
in a deeper sense, as he knew. He was a consciousness medi-
ating the raising of matter and spirit to the divine, beyond
the historical rites of the Christian Eucharist. Such was his
essential "priestly" office. Sammy had written two hundred
and sixty three pages on Teilhard's foresight. And yet, he still
could not fathom how, a century in advance, that man had
been able to sketch the paths along which modern sciences,
new technologies, ecology and even politics and religions were
arduously but surely converging. After three years of intense
study at Heythrop, he'd understood that the sacramental aspect
of his calling as a Jesuit priest had to be sacrificed, or outgrown,
rather. What the Catholic Church called the sacraments of Holy
Orders and of the Eucharist were noble but limited symbols
of merging with the divine. What primitive theology used to
call God was henceforth freed from the outdated categories of
gender, of personhood, of authority, of goodness and truth, and
even of singleness. What his elders had clumsily wrapped up
under the name of Christ was now revealed as Convergence. In

that sense, he had never been more Christian, more cosmic, as Teilhard eloquently put it: *"To live the cosmic life is to live with the dominating consciousness that each one of us is an atom of the mystical and cosmic body of Christ."* God was a process, not a person (neither one nor three of them); God was not one, but unification was God. Sammy had gradually understood that his destiny, his service to the world, lay in reaching beyond rituals, through cosmic communion with every being. Even though he had left Heythrop, he would be forever grateful to the Jesuits. Without them, he might never have been awakened.

There was, however, a fly in the ointment, or a grain of sand jamming the machinery. It was too small to worry Sammy, but dense enough to puzzle him. Why was it that the apparition of this benign "Fr Easy" (was that his real name?) a couple of hours ago had caused a hint of restlessness within his soul? While on his way down from the mountain he'd felt at peace as never before, and confirmed in his mission. But since the unexpected chat with that man, his conscience had become uneasy. What if Easy were a Jesuit in disguise? What if he'd been sent to test him? Sammy dismissed the suspicion of an attempt by his former colleagues to bring him back to their fold. They had always encouraged him. Even when he'd mentioned to his spiritual director that he could not feel God any longer in the Spiritual Exercises of St Ignatius, whilst drawing deep comfort from the Centering Prayer after the Buddhist fashion, the director had smiled with relief as if bearing witness to the maturing of his soul: "Now you're growing wings", he'd admitted. "Fly," he had added, "fly wherever the Spirit carries you!"

But now, to his dismay, his own spirit seemed to lead him backward, right back within the narrow parameters of Catholic sacramentality. Something was pricked or tickled in his soul, and he didn't know whether it was a superficial accident or a sign of a deeper change. Was it a gift from the Spirit, or a threat to his freedom? Sammy tried in vain to ignore a certain image implanted in his imagination after his conversation with Fr Easy. His eyes were drawn towards the wide mountain. He could not avoid seeing its long horizontal crest as an altar. So far, Teilhard would have agreed, of course. But to Sammy's embarrassment, the nearly full moon over the mountain seemed to superimpose in his imagination onto the white Host elevated by the priest during Mass, while the brighter stars shone as altar candles. His problem, he realised, was that the ritual elements suddenly felt more real than the material shapes, as if mountain and stars were mere echoes or symbols of a sacramental reality. That old priest meant to walk all the way to Uhuru Peak to offer Mass. He would sweat and freeze; he would suffer and get his gear all the way to the top, only to whisper a few words upon bread and wine. Sammy could not explain to himself why the Eucharistic ritual with which he was so familiar — even though he had not attended it for two years now — was obsoletely wooing his mind and heart. He was not consenting of course, but neither could he totally ignore the quixotic suggestion that the Host was, perhaps, more real than anything else. Should he fight against this regression? Or should he examine this awkward shrinking of his mental horizon? He was about to crouch in mindfulness posture before the "Eucharistic" moon when a dimmer light flashed, he noticed, inside Sue's hut. She was up, then, like him. Was it not a sign that he should go to her?

* * *

Fr Isidore was finding the ascent a bit more challenging than expected. It was the fourth day and Kibo Hut was in sight at 4,700 metres: their last stop before attempting to reach the summit, one last full kilometre up. It was past 5pm and the priest gave thanks for the insistence of his cousin Casimir and his altar server Sentwali. These young lads simply would not have let him undertake this trip without them. And now they walked before and behind him, making sure he didn't overdo it.

Most of all, they respected his silence. He'd meant this ascent as a pilgrimage and was keen on having mostly strangers around him. His prayer to God was to be able to let go . . . That wasn't easy. The path was very stony and eroded, so that he had to look carefully where he trod. This prevented him from glancing often at the laminated picture of his wife and son hanging from the strap of his backpack held in his left fist. Habimana would be 25 by now, a splendid young man. As to Naomi . . . She would also be 25. His wife would forever be 25.

After a three-hour nap at Kibo Hut, they started before midnight on the last stretch to the summit, first heading to Hans Meyer Cave. From there the path zigzagged up to Gillman's Point (5,681m) on the crater rim. Fr Isidore found it the most mentally and physically challenging part of the expedition. From Stella Point they encountered snow all the way on the remaining two-hour ascent to Uhuru Peak, which they reached around 7am. Breathing was hard at such altitude, and after the nearly eight-hour climb, too. The sky was clear and the moon full on this Monday, 28 September 2015. While other members of the group shouted with joy and took pictures, the priest moved aside and fell on his knees, his hands joined. He'd come as a pilgrim, not as a trekker. Below him, he pondered, spread the entire African continent, from Egypt to South Africa and from Morocco to Somalia. So many countries and peoples and souls. So many sins and so much suffering; and more graces, and prayers and merits. And he, Isidore Kabarebe, born in Rwanda some 55 years earlier, was part of it.

A portable altar was unfolded, Mass vestments and all liturgical items were set up by Casimir and the porters, while Sentwali buttoned a purposely oversized black cassock over his anorak, soon adding the white surplice. The small team's prayer for good weather had been answered as the temperature stayed at about +5 Celsius degrees (low 40's Fahrenheit), with no wind whatsoever (a rarity) during the hour spent at the top.

A handful of tourists stayed out of curiosity when holy Mass started, plus a number of apparently Catholic Tanzanian guides, glad to witness this unprecedented event. Having put on all his priestly vestments, Fr Easy faced the little altar and, ignoring the spectacular 360-degree panorama, attempted to make the first sign of the cross. Instead, having stood motionless for a few seconds, his right hand floating in the air, he collapsed on his knees, unable to proceed, while his back and shoulders shook with emotion. He was sobbing.

* * *

Sammy was not a little proud of himself. The shortest way to Uhuru Peak, the Umbwe Route, is considered to be very difficult and is the most challenging way up Mount Kilimanjaro. Due to the quick ascent, Umbwe does not provide the necessary stages for altitude acclimatization to a fifty percent drop in oxygen compared with the atmosphere at sea level. But having climbed the mountain with his rugby team over the past week, Sammy's body was fit and ready, enabling him to make it all the way up, unlike most of his undertrained fellow climbers who had overestimated their ability to acclimatize. Physical exertion was a timely diversion for the young film-director after his bitter disappointment at Honey Badger Lodge.

No use brooding any further. Sammy had failed to see it coming. That was all. Yes, there had been a first hug two years previous, when he had evoked the spiritual value of Steve's suffering and death. Recently widowed, Sue was emotionally vulnerable and making Sammy's acquaintance at a Heythrop-sponsored fundraising event had unveiled before her eyes the horizons of the supernatural, until then unknown to her. They had met more frequently as their friendship deepened. In fairness, the kiss last year didn't count; it was an accident, a faux-pas (whose, he wasn't sure). Still, that was when he'd first experienced sentimental attraction. Man, it was kind of cosmic!

Since then, he had reached the conclusion that the Spirit was leading him towards marriage with Sue. Together, they would converge towards the Omega Point. Sue had laughed at this formulation without really understanding it. Sammy had assumed she approved, as Teilhard surely did—or did he?

"Five-minute pause, everyone!" The guide's shout interrupted his thoughts. Umbwe Gate was far behind the trekkers by then. Further down, Sammy caught a last glimpse of the villages and coffee and banana plantations through which they had been driven on their approach. The trail now ascended sharply on a forestry track. To think that just a few days earlier, he was holding Sue's hand—briefly towing her on an occasion when she'd looked breathless—on their ascent along the easier Marangu Route. Reaching the highest point in Africa together was meant as a catalyst in their relationship. He'd carried a ring against his chest to propose to Sue at Uhuru Peak, but found himself too busy filming the rugby game instead, while secretly unsure of her reaction. Back at Honey Badger Lodge, when he'd walked to her hut that last night, finding her in no need of his company, he'd retreated unseen, his sweaty fist cemented around the black velvet box of his proposal ring. The following morning, at brunch, a jubilant Harry had announced their engagement before the forty players and staff. Sophrology ethos and a sleepless night (and among other reasons, Harry's 6.4 feet and 94kg), had dissuaded Sammy from expressing his fury verbally, even less so physically. Along with the crowd, he'd managed to cheer the radiant couple, closing his eyes when they'd kissed. Nobody seemed to pay much attention when he said that he would not fly back with the players and crew later that morning but would meet them in Manchester the following week instead, as he "wished to film wildlife at the nearby Serengeti National Park." Then they'd gone.

He spent the afternoon alone. After half an hour in his favourite Qigong posture, the Soaring Crane, he was even more frustrated than before and resorted to the less demanding Wild Goose position, alas, with no more success. Finally selecting a simpler method to dispel the burdensome illusion of selfhood, he got drunk that evening and stayed in bed nearly twenty-four hours. After supper, going online for the first time in nearly two days, he managed avoiding any site connected with the latest achievement of the Warburton Rugby Team. Glancing at the Kilimanjaro in the distance above his laptop screen, he fought valiantly against bitterness: no, this splendid mountain was not Mount Doom, the theatre of his heart's sacrifice, the altar of his good faith spurned by a superficial woman (she thought Karl Rahner was a rugby coach)... Rather, the roof of Africa was a cosmic catalyst where multiple paths converged, crossed — some going their separate ways, admittedly. There was, for instance, this strong porter who had carried his two cameras with a smile all the way to the summit. There was that funny priest he'd never meet again and whose...

This was the exact moment, Sammy later reckoned, when the thought of Fr Easy first came back to his jaded mind. Strangely, it immediately brought with it the absurd suggestion of ascending the mountain again, there to attend his Mass at Uhuru Peak. What folly! That would be much worse than getting drunk. Making friends with Fr Easy was one thing, but supporting his sacramental view of the numinous was another. However, the man was also a rugby fan, wasn't he? Puzzled, Sammy decided to look him up despite not knowing his surname. There was very little about Rwandan rugby, until a picture came up of one Isidore Kabarebe chatting with Francois Pienaar of the Springboks in 1994. Apparently, Isidore was promoting rugby as a way of overcoming ethnic tensions. Whereas Pienaar had made that hope come true with his World Cup victory the following year in South Africa, the civil war in Rwanda had crushed Isidore's dream. It was all that came up online. Sammy was about to give up, when he tried the keywords "Fr Easy" instead of "Isidore." Hundreds of hits led to a YouTube video posted in 2007. It was an address spoken in clumsy German at a *Justice and Peace* Congress organised by the University of Tübingen. Fr Easy was introduced as a survivor of the Rwandan genocide and an apostle of ethnic reconciliation. The English subtitles were eloquent:

"My friends, my Superior insisted that I should speak to you today. Forgive me because I am not a theologian, as most of you are. Yes, it is true that I lost my wife and my son in the massacres. Many more men did. Some were working in the fields when the others arrived and I...I was on the rugby pitch with our young men. You see, I used to be a rugby coach. No longer, though. Meanwhile, our wives and children were praying in the village church and... Forgive me. I don't think I need to tell more about this. I am...I am amputated. You see my body whole. Look at my hands. Look at my feet. You think, this man he is okay. This man he has all his limbs. Why does he say that he is amputated? My friends, my wife was my flesh and she was cut off from me. My son was our flesh, and he was chopped off from us. We were one family and now they're gone. And now I am left with my soul chopped off, even though my body is okay. And yet, we must forgive. We..."

Fr Easy paused, visibly overwhelmed by emotion. As a sympathetic diversion and as an encouragement, the VIP's seating on the front row started clapping, immediately followed by the vast amphitheatre. The priest went on:

"Please, don't applaud, because what have I done? I let them be chopped off. I tried to live on. I became a priest. Why? Because I hoped to offer up. I hope to help and to heal. I try, but it's difficult. Once, I came across one of the men who'd killed my family, my village. I know he was in it. I... Anyway. You know there were also priests who supported the massacres. I am so ashamed. Yes, some priests approved the killing of innocent people. But my friends, that was thirteen years ago. I must tell you something else. Something that is happening here and now. It will make you sad. I am sorry. Your country was kind to me. I studied here in Germany for three years, sent by my Superior from our community's motherhouse in Tanzania. I had good teachers. How beautiful is our Catholic faith. Jesus, the only Saviour of all men. The Immaculate Virgin Mary, our Mother. The sacraments and the all-pure Church, the Bride of Christ. And yet, when I see everybody leaving the Church here in Germany — 217,000 last year — I am so sad. When I see those who remain try to change what we have always believed, it breaks my heart. When I see, please forgive me, when I see even some of our Fathers the Bishops write things which are not at all in the catechism, I think, perhaps the journalist he made a mistake or he didn't understand what the Father Bishop really said."

Sammy was not surprised when two people in the front row walked out. Although, they might have had very good reasons. Fr Easy continued:

"But my friends, it does not change the outcome. Souls are chopped off. The living limbs of the Church are cut off from the all-pure Bride of Christ. And we, we priests, are doing it. When, you wonder. When do priests do that terrible thing? We chop off souls from the mystical Body of Christ, His beloved Church, when we teach falsity, calculated ambiguity. We chop off souls when we remain silent in the face of danger in morality and doctrine, instead of guiding our flock in safety. We chop off souls when we lead luxurious and immoral lives, scandalising our good people. We chop off souls when we force abortion and contraception upon the peoples of Africa, because we say these people need education, civilisation. Then, my friends, our homilies become machetes. Our Sunday bulletins, they become machetes. Our diocesan circular letters also they become machetes. Our words and our silences twist the Good News of Salvation in Christ and through His Cross. Our words and our silences, they prevent even non-Catholics from hearing Christ. We cut their ears off, so they can't listen, they can't believe and be saved. Perhaps we mean well. But we still cause harm, my friends. Remember on Maundy Thursday, in the garden, Simon Peter, he struck Malchus with his machete in Gethsemane. Peter meant well, to save Jesus. But Jesus is the Saviour, not we priests. And Jesus, what did he do then? He healed Malchus; he put his ear back on him. Let us pray, my friends, that we priests may drop our machetes and take up our crucifixes instead. And please God, please Mother Mary, the dead limbs, they will live again. The children of Jesus, they will wake up and come back. And the Bride of Jesus, Holy Mother Church, she will smile again. Thank you."

A veiled nun and a young man in a cassock stopped applauding when realising they were the only ones. Sammy saw an elegant woman with short hair rise from the VIP's front row and shake hand with Fr Easy who moved aside from the ambo where she took his place.

"Thank you so much Fr Easy for having come from distant Africa to deliver this moving testimony in our rather tricky German language. What if I had to lecture in Swahili, or in Latin for that matter! Allow me to reformulate the gist of your speech with enhanced idiomatic accuracy for those among us who might have missed some of your wisdom. You reminded us of the need for a shift of paradigm from a totemic ecclesiology, shaped by the primal notion of bodily integrity, to an evolutive understanding of what it means to be Church in our technological era, when the human body improved by mechanical devices already buds with nanoprotheses, and soon will flower into blessed transhumanism. We agree with you, Fr Easy, when you point at the constraints of the Pauline ecclesiology marked by the archaic and machistic anthropology of antiquity. Assuredly, modern developments call for a Church no more amputated from the contributions of any human of good will; a Church welcoming every race, gender, creed and culture for what they are, not for what our neo-colonial reflexes would induce us to turn them into."

Sammy had caught some repressed smiles on the faces of the VIP's, who now openly grinned and started clapping. The chairwoman went on:

"In addition, may I add that God is the God of surprises indeed, since he enriched us with your thought-provoking theological input when we expected a presentation on the merits of rugby to foster reconciliation among rival tribes. No one in this learned audience will object, surely, if I quote for the purpose of illustration the greatest contribution of one Joseph Ratzinger to German theology, in his June 3, 1978 Munich address on football: '*Sport is based on positive values: as training for life and as a stepping over from our daily life in the direction of our lost Paradise.*' To conclude, in my capacity as chairperson of this *Justice and Peace* convention, let me present Fr Easy with this genuine rugby ball which will be auctioned later on to raise funds for peace efforts in his dear country of Uganda — sorry, of Rwanda. I realise however that we are now late on schedule, so that I will leave it to our sponsors to approach him directly during the refreshments and offer their contributions if they wish, while we prepare to welcome in fifteen minutes — please be punctual — our guest of honour the Venerable Hu Shan, special envoy of His Holiness the Dalai Lama, for his master conference on 'Zen and Sufism, a Model of Religious Convergence for the West.'"

* * *

Crouched down in the snow, on his knees before his makeshift altar, Fr Easy was asking God to be able to let go. He had torn from its string around his neck the picture of his wife and son, but he still had to slip it under the corporal, on the altar. However, he couldn't. That last gesture was a definitive parting with them, he knew. This Mass was for them, and for Rwanda, and for Africa. All along the ascent, and for years past, he had begged for the grace of accepting the tragedy. He thought he had, by God's grace. How could his mostly Catholic country have fallen into such genocidal frenzy? In his mind, he had reasoned it through. Sure, the question of evil; God's ability to draw a greater good from the worst atrocities. But now, when examining his conscience on the top of Mount Kilimanjaro, he knew that deep inside, he yet had to achieve a full, unconditional surrender to God's Providence. That was easier said than done. He'd read many times the Book of Job in the Old Testament, and had tried to learn from that saintly man's wisdom and humility. A big difference though, Job's wife was very much alive, albeit trying to undermine her husband's hope. But his wife was dead... His Naomi, who'd been his hope... Many times he'd imagined himself on the roof of Africa, elevating the Divine Victim, the Lamb of God who takes away the sins of the world. He had resolved to mentally gather into the Host and offer to God the Father every sin to be expiated, every suffering to be healed and every fear to be cast away. And now, having at long last reached the summit, he found the Eucharistic offering too heavy a task. Lurking in some remote corner of his conscience, a wicked thought seemed to spread: that of uselessness. He tried to ignore it, but the temptation grew bolder. "Pointless," it whispered. "Hollow," it declared. What could that rite achieve? Men would be men; they would find new weapons if machetes rusted.

Meanwhile, Sammy had been regularly speaking over the phone with his former camera porter who was now climbing with Fr Easy's team along the slower Marangu Route. Thanks to the porter's updates, Sammy had been able to catch up and reach Uhuru Peak on time for the Mass at dawn. The young man wasn't sure what exactly he was seeking there. He'd just felt that the Spirit was leading him back onto the mountain. However, not wishing to make himself known, he'd stood at some distance with some tourists, behind the little altar facing east, on the edge of a cliff. He'd been concerned to see the old priest collapse and nearly jumped to his rescue. But two young men — one his altar server apparently — were already at his sides, trying to lift him up.

*   *   *

You can't beat Diani Beach. Nothing like eleven miles of white sand along turquoise shallow water, stretching by the shade of luxuriant palm trees, with comparatively few tourists in that season. Sammy had decided to treat himself to a couple of days break. The past month had been frantically busy, as he was putting the finishing touches to his postgraduate dissertation on "Documenting Conflict in Africa," at the Communication and Film Department of the Technical University of Mombasa in Kenya. By the skin of his teeth, he'd met the 19th July submission deadline, thank God. His study compared famous documentaries portraying conflicts in Africa in the fields of ecology, racism, healthcare, and religion. *Virunga* depicted the murderous schemes of oil companies coveting gorilla territory at the national park in Congo. Sammy recalled his embarrassment when meeting with the wife of the park's director who lived in Nairobi. Despite being a third-generation renowned anthropologist, Lidwina Seymour had first seemed unaware of Teilhard's reputation as a fellow scientist until, with a rather inauspicious smile, she'd commented: "Teilhard de Chardin, was he not that priest involved in the 1913 Piltdown Man hoax, an alleged proof of evolution? My grandfather strongly doubted that the lower jaw really belonged to the same individual as the skull." Sammy had prudently steered the conversation back to her husband, the Virunga park director, a Belgian prince who'd survived assassination by the hitmen of an oil company and whose documentary could soon be turned into a Hollywood film (Leonardo Di Caprio owned the rights). *16th Man*

showed the historical facts of the 1995 Rugby World Cup victory
in South Africa. Fr Easy had obtained for Sammy an inter-
view with Francois Pienaar of the Springboks. *Strings Attached*
exposed the neo-colonialism of Western organisations in Africa,
such as Marie Stopes International which was promoting drastic
reduction of the fertility of the poor. Sammy had found his
neutral stance on this issue no longer sustainable after meeting
with Obianuju Ekeocha, the young authoress of that documentary. Finally, the 2015 video by Islamic State of Iraq and the
Levant showed the assassination of twenty-one Egyptian Copts
in Libya. Including this last item wasn't Sammy's idea. He'd
argued with his tutor that it belonged to the category of pro-
paganda films rather than documentaries. In the end, he agreed
that it further enriched the diversity of angles for his study.

Reclining under the shade of a beach hut, Sammy gazed at
the turquoise horizon. Up to then, he'd seen very little of the
idyllic Kenyan coastline by the Indian Ocean. Right across from
Diani Beach, a mere 2,700 miles as the crow flies, lay his native
Goa. He had visited there again the past year to see his family.
They had insisted on his return home for good but he wasn't
ready. It had been a wise decision, he felt, not to settle back in
London either after the Kilimanjaro ordeal, already four years
previous. As a compromise, he'd worked two years in film production for tour operators in the African Great Lakes Region.
Then, two years ago, he'd found this postgraduate fellowship
in Mombasa, as a steppingstone between Britain and India.
He was feeling at peace with himself and with God. In a way,
he'd stopped waiting for signs. He prayed, and even went to
Mass and confession. Without seeking it, he'd found again the
Catholic faith of his youth and had managed to keep his heart
free to hear the call. He'd asked God whether he should get
back on track for the priesthood but there had been no clear
answer, although his parents were still hoping that he would
return to the Jesuits. Sammy looked at his wrist, smiling. That

Fr Easy had an acute sense of observation. How had he noticed that the three nails were missing from his Jesuit tattoo? The sunburst shone around the *IHS*, but no nails of Christ's crucifixion showed at the bottom. Sammy had meant to have them added, if at all, once ordained. Thinking of it, it'd been over a year since he'd last heard from the Rwandan priest. Sammy appreciated that he'd never tried to push him towards the priesthood, even after their awkward encounter at Uhuru Peak. The young man hadn't felt anything in particular up there. He'd just been glad to have come to the Mass. Attending that sacred event had somehow cleansed the mountain and his memory from the shame of his failed engagement on that same location a few days earlier. He was about to take some pictures which Fr Easy might like to keep when he realised that it wasn't the time. That kind of action didn't need to be consigned to digital memory and it was more respectful not to post it online either. He had downplayed Fr Easy's comment on their return at Honey Badger Lodge: "On spotting you nearby, I regained my strength to offer that Mass." At the time, Sammy hadn't understood the Latin words spoken thrice by the exhausted priest holding the small host towards the young men on the snow-capped summit: *"Domine non sum dignus ut intres sub tectum meum . . . "* Well, it had been four years since he'd left the roof of Africa and now, 5,895 metres lower, here on sea level, turquoise waves awaited him!

Sammy stood up for a swim. On his way out of the hut, his eyes caught on the visitors' notice board a coloured pattern which stirred some yet unidentified memory. *"The 2019 Diani Beach Touch Rugby was held on the weekend 13–14th July, after a week of torrential rain and high winds. The event started with testing conditions for many of the visiting teams on Friday evening. Forty Thieves Beach Bar, Diani, saw 28 teams from 4 nations with some top Kenyan teams competing. But the sun shone the entire Sunday including for the final game."* Pictures depicted young men in orange sports shirts, kneeling around the ball, their dark skin contrasting aesthetically with the blue sea and the white sand. Sammy laboured to identify what similar sporting event by a beach had impressed his memory. Could it have been the famous sequence in *Chariots of Fire*, when athletes are seen running barefoot on wet sand as waves break close by? Not quite, because those were wearing white, whereas the sportsmen in his memory wore orange. Sammy left the shade of the thatched palm roof and ventured upon the burning sand, still searching his memory. It hit him near the water. The winning team, of course, with twenty-one players on either side of the contest. On their knees by the sea, some wearing their orange overalls while as many masked giants unsheathed daggers from under their black jackets. He remembered now. These eerie "All Blacks" thought they'd won on that Libyan beach in 2015. Little did they know. Oblivious of his dip, the young man knelt down in the sand, facing home across the sea. A more exhilarating swim was offered him, he suddenly knew.

God willing, Sammy Prabhu would not fail to respond.

VI

The Meteorite Mystery

(2017, PORTUGAL)

S UBDEACON YAROSLAV WAS GLAD TO stretch his long legs. The decrepit bus had covered the distance from Lviv in less than forty hours, with just a couple of breaks at petrol stations. He yawned again after his short night, spent on board to save hotel costs. Soon they would all get to the cheap hostel booked for the forty-six pilgrims (and hopefully take a shower). But before that, the Divine Liturgy would have to be celebrated. Yaroslav kept walking to and fro along the vestibule between the lavatory and the sacristy, waiting for their guide and translator. His attention was caught by a singular gathering, visible on the screen to his side. Half a dozen religious delegates were sitting in a semi-circle. It looked like an ecumenical prayer meeting. Yaroslav knew those often happened, here in the West. Apprehensive and intrigued, he decided to check if all that he had heard was true. Subtitles helped indentify the speakers and translated their interventions for foreigners like him. Obviously, in this Centennial year, not only Ukrainians but many more nationalities flocked to the celebrated shrine.

* * *

With a modest smile, Rabbi Isaac thanked the participants for inviting him to speak first "out of deference for the earliest monotheistic religion."

"In her flight with her husband, Lot's wife turned back to look at the heavenly fire falling upon Sodom. Why, O Edith, did you disobey the angels' order? They had commanded: *Escape for thy life; look not behind thee, neither stay thou in all the Plain; escape to the mountain, lest thou be swept away.* In punishment, the Almighty changed her into a pillar of salt. It was a warning to all men to look forward in faith and hope, in the direction given by the Most High."

Rabbi Isaac paused, twisting his white sidelocks or *payots* with his fingers. He knew that all eyes were focused on him, all hearts awaiting his interpretation. With a little smile, he finally uttered:

"Edith. I look at this monolithic shape emerging from the floor and I see Edith. This is a pillar of salt. Its rugged aspect and its compact structure evoke the unfortunate fate of Lot's wife. It is a stela, depicting impious nostalgia for past sins and complacency. It is *Edith*."

The various dignitaries remained silent for a little while, meditating on the wisdom of the rabbi. Having thanked Rabbi Isaac, the coordinator glanced hesitatingly at the next participant, Imam Husayn, who cleared his throat and affirmed in a loud voice:

"A bad woman she was, disobeying her husband Lut, Ibrahim's god-fearing nephew. Fire upon her and upon her imitators! But Rabbi Isaac did not look far enough back. Long before Lut's wife, I see Adam and Eve, to whom the Almighty sent from heaven a large black stone to sacrifice upon. Several years before his first revelation, the Prophet recognised the Black Stone in Mecca. Since then all of us Muslims venerate it in its silver frame, cemented in *al-Rukn al-Aswad*, at the east corner of the Kaaba. The dimensions of your stone are similar to those of the original Black Stone. I see in it homage to the first order given by Allah to offer sacrifice."

Imam Husayn spoke with some agitation. Now settling his *taqiyah*, or cap, on his thick-haired skull, he looked at a paper in his hand, adding:

"Clumsy homage, I must say, not agreeable to *Ar-Raḥīm* the Merciful. But a stepping stone nonetheless, since this place belongs to our princess, outrageously abducted by the Crusader Gonçalo Hermigues; and to her it shall return."

The coordinator nodded in appreciation, before inviting the next representative to share her views. The Honourable Iyalawo Ositola stood up and smoothed the wrinkles of her colourful West African dress. "Any members of the animist religions will recognise this stone. It clearly belongs to Senegambian stone circles in Central Senegal. Judging by its brown colour and the ritual scar inflicted horizontally all along its front, I can affirm that our ancestors once set it as part of a double circle in Sine Ngayene. Why, I must ask, was our religious artefact removed from its original setting? Why do Westerners think they can scavenge our sacred patrimony?"

Her brass and ivory necklace now shaking, the Honourable Iyalawo Ositola suddenly looked as if in a trance. Some representatives glanced at each other, wondering whether things were about to get out of control. She sung the following words in a sort of antediluvian rhythm, sending shivers in the marrow of Rabbi Isaac, while Imam Husayn frowned intensely:

"If you are men of faith, you will agree that I, an Iyalawo, a Yoruba priestess, must ask for the stone to be returned. You will be wise if you start placating the spirits protecting this stone, or Olodumare, our Supreme Creator, will change you into b... Into filthy bw..." The priestess fell on her knees with a great shriek and remained silent and motionless. After a few seconds, as if awakening from stupor, the coordinator snapped his fingers to a couple of robust-looking security staff who removed the priestess into the sacristy.

Since no one seemed willing to speak next, Professor Eduardo Bosch tightened his light grey tie and crossed his legs on his chair with humorous relief:

"For a moment, I feared that the Honourable Ositola might have been turned into a pillar of salt. Having listened to the fascinating religious interpretations of the valued participants, I will now venture a scientific hypothesis. As a meteoricist, I must admit my bewilderment when first entering here and sighting this object. It resembles so perfectly the Hoba meteorite that I first assumed it was a purpose-made replica. The learned participants are fully cognizant of the fact that 2.7-metre long Hoba, the largest known intact meteorite as a single piece, lies not far from Grootfontein, in the Otjozondjupa Region of Namibia. The name 'Hoba' comes from a Khoekhoegowab word meaning 'gift.' But I can hear your objection: how could I call Hoba 'intact' since a 165-kg fragment of it is on display at the Lord Maurice Egerton collection in Tatton Park in England? If, like me, you have read Professor Sarah Bothwell's thesis on this topic, you remember with no little relief that the Tatton fragment actually belongs to the Gideon meteorite, not to the Hoba. As you all have guessed, this indisputable conclusion brings us back elliptically to... To?"

The participants failed to provide and answer, having all at once turned their heads towards the sacristy out of which the priestess emerged, looking more composed. With the condescending patience of a veteran lecturer, Professor Eduardo Bosch ignored the distraction of his audience and stated:

"This indisputable conclusion brings us back elliptically to the Honourable Ositola's question: why do we Westerners take away precious African stones? In my scientific opinion, however, no one carried the aerolite, in whose impressive presence we presently sit, all the way over here in Portugal. The impact crater surrounding it demonstrates that the object simply fell from heaven. On our side of it, indeed, we can observe the deep impact rift running parallel to the meteorite, even with flowers growing out of it. The impact occurred probably 50,000 years ago. At the time, this extraterrestrial object would have sat amidst raised rims and floors lower in elevation than the surrounding terrain. Over time, wind and rain levelled the soil around it. Its velocity must have been low — no more than half a kilometre per second, or it would have caused a much wider impact crater. No doubt it soon became the focus of some pre-Christian worship, until the original pagan temple was turned into this Catholic one, which explains — in case you wondered — why there is no hole in the roof: the meteorite didn't fall through it, but occupied this site long before the church was erected."

The coordinator shook the hand of Professor Eduardo Bosch with visible emotion. His interpretation of the mysterious object clearly was the one he preferred. Science offered him spiritual emancipation in a way none of the religious hypotheses had, so far. Having succeeded in withdrawing his right hand from the effusive grasp of his host, Professor Eduardo Bosch undertook to wipe his rimless glasses.

The coordinator then bowed ceremoniously towards the next speaker. Was there a hint of fear in the host's utter seriousness when introducing Baron Pombal, Worshipful Master of the Grand Orient of Lusitania? If so, it was promptly dispelled by the Baron's jovial countenance. He returned the coordinator's bow with casual distinction and, having tied around his waist his ceremonial apron, announced:

"What could I ever add to the insightful explanations offered by my illustrious friends Rabbi Isaac, Imam Husayn, the Honourable Iyalawo Ositola and Professor Eduardo Bosch? Truly, it seems to me that faiths and science were meant to meet in this sacred location. It is the mission of Freemasonry to promote this enlightening synthesis. Dear woman and men of good will, let us give thanks to the Great Architect who convened us around his corner stone. We, the heirs of King Solomon, wish to restore the fallen temple, to the everlasting glory of the Supreme Being."

While Rabbi Isaac smiled complacently at the Hebrew characters embroidered on the triangular apron, Imam Husayn looked with disgust at the golden frills hanging along the edges of the vestment. The imam deeply disapproved of modern men performing domestic chores such as cooking or washing up — all

womanly duties—and the frills only increased the disgrace. But
Baron Pombal went on apparently unoffended:

"Here we are, happily meeting as friends, as we sit around
the great stone, flanked by its three candlesticks. Why *three*
candlesticks and not four or two, you may wonder? Why one
candleless angle to this brown parallelepiped, apparently hin-
dering the expected symmetry? This distinctive feature appears
in all our temples. It refers to the three great lights, the Sun,
the Moon, and the Master of the Lodge. As the Sun rules the
day, and the Moon governs the night, so ought the Master rule
and govern his lodge with equal regularity. Mine is a heavy
responsibility, honourable friends, as I strive to set the best
example for my brethren. But when I look at this square altar
with the three candlesticks at its angles, I remember that I can
rely on a tradition of several centuries improved by each of
my predecessors to serve the public interest with ever greater
dedication. Famously, when the hydra of superstition threatened
this forlorn village in 1917, my colleague Oliveira Santos 'Tin-
smith,' the then-Administrator of Ourem, applied the resources
of his pedagogical heart to rescue poor peasant children from
medieval gloom. We continue his work."

The coordinator thanked the participants, assuring the audience that the basilica was a house of encounter for all traditions.
He then invited a Catholic priest in attendance to offer a final
prayer of thanksgiving. The priest made a slow sign of the
cross and began:

"Dear pilgrims, as we give thanks for the happy completion of
the restoration of the basilica of Our Lady of the Holy Rosary
in Fatima to its pristine condition, we..."

*   *   *

On seeing Maksym enter the sacristy with João, their Portuguese guide, Subdeacon Yaroslav yawned and left the vestibule where he'd stood idle for the past fifteen minutes. He had

been watching the video presentation on the Centenary restoration of the Holy Rosary Basilica played on a visitors' screen. Despite the English subtitles, Yaroslav had not understood all that was said. He scratched his beard nervously, hoping that the guide would be able to explain to the Shrine sacristan Fr Oleksiy's requirements to offer the Divine Liturgy. On arrival earlier, he had started spreading an altar cloth and setting up liturgical items when the sacristan had interrupted him with determination, gesturing (or threatening?) to telephone someone, perhaps the Cardinal? — while pointing with insistence at the empty sanctuary behind him. It was now past 5am and time was running short to complete the ceremony before the official opening of the basilica at 6am. Everything had worked so well until then. With the drivers taking turns, the bus had reached Fatima before dawn: quite a feat. Now the forty-six Ukrainian pilgrims — some still a bit drowsy — were anxious to attend the Divine Liturgy.

When João walked back in his direction across the sacristy, Yaroslav needed no interpreter to understand he had failed. The Portuguese guide confirmed that the sacristan remained inflexible. Yes, he was well aware of the fact that the Ukrainian Catholic Church was in full communion with Rome. No, he'd not wished to check Fr Oleksiy's *celebret*. Indeed, he'd acknowledged the booking for the ceremony confirmed in writing eleven weeks earlier. He was even the one who'd stated that the Shrine had demonstrated great flexibility in opening at 4:30am, ninety minutes before the official group Masses, for the sake of the liturgical peculiarities of the Ukrainian rite. So, what was the issue? Was there such an affluence of pilgrims that the longer Oriental ceremony should have to be curtailed? Surely not, since not a soul had been met along the streets or on the vast esplanade, as the group had staggered its way from the bus, Yaroslav had noticed, despite it being October 2017. Even now, the basilica was empty.

What the sacristan adamantly denied, João reported with considerable embarrassment, was the choice of an altar. How? It was not as if altars were lacking in this older basilica. In addition to the main one dedicated to the Dormition of the Blessed Virgin Mary, no fewer than fourteen others could be seen, seven along either side wall of the nave. Thus, there were fifteen altars in total, one for each mystery of the Holy Rosary, each of them resting against marble panels and gradines, with a fine carved relief of the Annunciation, or of the Visitation, of the Nativity etc., looking nearly as evocative as the icons on the iconostasis, back home. When João pointed at a rough cubic shape in the middle of the sanctuary, Maksym did not understand. The object looked as if freshly hewn from a quarry before being transported to a workshop where the sculpting would begin. João explained that the Divine Liturgy had to be celebrated upon the modern cube, or not at all. Yaroslav could not believe such an arbitrary demand. Why on earth not use the high altar, where God was present in the tabernacle? Alternatively, why not use the side altars with their very relevant depictions of the Holy Rosary, in this centennial year, when pilgrims from the entire world were coming to recite the prayer commanded by the Blessed Virgin to the three young seers? But the main obstacle was, planted with flowers, the long slit in the marble at the foot of the cube, forbidding the celebrant to stand on that side facing east. Holy Mass facing west, *against* the people instead of *ahead* of them? How could Fr Oleksiy ever offer the holy Sacrifice facing the congregation rather than the Orient, where the rising sun prefigured the glorious return of the Risen Christ!

Deeply shocked by such inhospitality, and repressing a surge of anger against what he ascribed to a flawed Western theology, Yaroslav made his way towards the side aisle where he had left Fr Oleksiy prostrate on his knees half an hour earlier. To think that this heroic priest had suffered radiation sickness after ministering to victims of the 1986 catastrophe in Chernobyl, and was now denied the right to worship according to his own tradition in the very basilica of Our Lady! He would warn the priest against the modern block that seemed to have sucked sacredness out of the fifteen altars, all suddenly declared "unfit for Mass" and degraded into mere shelves for plastic plants, while that rough stone now claimed liturgical monopoly. But behind the pews, the shape of the man of God had vanished! Yaroslav looked in vain in the nave and even outside the church on the esplanade: still empty. Back in the sacristy, he finally caught sight of Fr Oleksiy... vesting. What was happening, Subdeacon Yaroslav wondered? The old priest gave him a fatherly smile, saying: "Please arrange our items for Holy Mass where the sacristan said. I will stand on the flowers' side, never mind the gap. As for the stone, let's assume that it fell from the sky during the miracle of the dancing star. We'll offer the Son on a block of sun."

VII

Congestion on the Silk Road
(2019, BURMA)

"AN INVASION, YOUR EXCELLENCY: that's what it is, even though these Chinese refugees are called 'workers.' For the sake of our copper mine, the Chinese will do anything to take control of Shwekai, never mind that this territory has been part of Burma for centuries." Fr Camille Malung crossed his arms as he stood in front of the mahogany desk in the office of the Right Reverend Pius Thaung, Bishop of Hpagok. The room had air-conditioning, thankfully, to shelter the two clerics from the 38°C heat (with 81% humidity) in early July 2019; it was also equipped with a dehumidifier as the Bishop had poor lungs. Fr Malung looked at the heavy rain in the courtyard of Bishop's House: "If only the Chinese mining company hadn't polluted our soil five years ago, forcing our hard-working Burmese farmers to desert the land of their fathers! Sweet Lord, why are we so close to the Chinese border?"

"Pray, Fr Malung, pray. But we cannot afford to be political about this. Our own Burmese government has now allowed four-thousand Chinese to relocate into the somehow insalubrious district of Shwekai, still part of the Hpagok diocese. We know that they are being exiled on religious grounds — one third being Muslims and the other two thirds Catholics. Now, Rome wants priests for these poor people."

"Forgive me Excellency, but we can't play into the hands of Beijing. The Communists hope to kill two birds with one stone. They threatened these Chinese Catholics with mass deportation inland unless they 'willingly' migrated across our border as 'workers' with their families. Having depopulated Shwekai through pollution five years ago, Beijing now argues that their 'workers' will accept any labour which our locals are not able to perform on *our* land."

"Fr Malung, *per* our Government's agreement with China, these workers *are* now Burmese citizens. They aren't Chinese anymore, and we must support them. Furthermore, our four churches in the Shwekai deanery have been barely used over the past five years. Much as I regret that our good Burmese Catholics had to relocate farther away, we must welcome this unexpected arrival of Catholic brethren from the East."

The conversation was interrupted by "*Chairman Meow*," the episcopal cat, who leapt onto his master's desk and ordered soya milk. Fr Malung noted that naming a pet after the founder of Communist China, even by way of a pun, could be seen as "political" indeed by the Chinese neighbours across the nearby border. But he knew that ingratiating himself with the four-pawed "*Chairman*" was a sure way of securing the benevolence of his superior. To the bishop's credit, the priest admitted, for once the pet's command (or pest's) for an added breakfast had been disobeyed. "*Chairman Meow*" stared with consternation at His Lordship of Hpagok, whose training into feline submission was still so embarrassingly defective. Stroking the cat with a seemingly affectionate hand, Fr Malung went on.

"Your Excellency always asks me to speak freely. Forgive me, but, while I agree in principle with filling our pews, even with Chinese, I wonder how genuinely Catholic these refugees are. For all we know, many of them could be Communist agents, and the others are underground Catholics with no connection with the Holy See for decades. Having followed rogue bishops for years, they might not even know who the Pope is, let alone obey him. I hear that most of that lot follow the preconciliar Latin Mass, as if the new Chinese missal had never reached them. In truth, they may have no clue even about Vatican II."

"You just put your finger on it, Fr Malung. Thank you for your frankness, which is welcome, as always. My estimate is that two thousand of these our new fellow-Burmese use the normal Chinese missal. Three of our priests in Shwekai speak enough Chinese and will thus care for these families. Only six hundred souls follow the old Latin missal. Thankfully for those, the Holy Father has fully authorized the preconciliar Mass since 2007, twelve years ago. The Vatican document states that the older missal 'was never officially abrogated.' I don't recall reading about it. As my vicar general, you are welcome to learn how to offer that old Mass for them. But if you fear the imposition on your busy schedule, our mission to these souls, however awkward, is to give them pastors according to their hearts. I will put you in touch with Mgr Phang in Rome. (We studied together at the Salesianum.) He will update you on the various traditionalist options. Please find some sound clergy based on his advice, but remember our government's stipulation as per their agreement with Beijing: 'No *Chinese* priest is allowed to minister to these new Burmese Catholics.' They must be foreigners, if not Burmese."

* * *

Deacon Symanski parked the brand-new Hyundai Creta at a little distance from St Joseph's Church. It was an elegant nineteenth-century building of a light crimson colour, located in a residential area of Shwekai City, Shan State. The church had its own car park, but better not let their shiny rental SUV give an inaccurate impression of wealth (the old parish Toyota was simply too unreliable for such a long drive). In anticipation of the nine-hour journey, he had left Mandalay with his Dominican superior the evening before, after Vespers on the feast of the Assumption, stopping on the way for a few hours' rest in a car park. They'd managed to avoid most of the torrential afternoon rain. Auspiciously, their trip from the centre of Burma had started under the protection of the Mother of God and would conclude on 17th August with the feast of St

Hyacinth of Poland, the Dominican patron of their fast-growing community. Fr Kowalski smiled: "Praying the Rosary is the best way to drive into a city for the very first time. Look Michal, the church is bigger than I thought. Now, we're too early for our appointment and you must be exhausted. Are you sure you don't want to take a nap before getting in?"

But the young deacon was eager to see the building (also, their lavatory might *not* be out of order, like the one at the petrol station forty kilometres earlier). Forgetting that the pair must have been the only Polish-speakers in that north-east district of Burma, Fr Kowalski whispered: "Let's walk in then, Michal, but very discreetly. It's essential that we should not attract attention since the Bishop hasn't yet publicised our taking over."

Shutting the door quietly behind them, the two religious knelt at the back of the church. A Mass in Burmese was on. After five years running his community's parish in Mandalay, Fr Kowalski spoke just enough Burmese to preach and hear confessions, but Deacon Symanski still needed to type and read aloud his entire homilies, underlining the difficult words and the syllables to be stressed. It took him longer than Fr Kowalski to identify the First Reading as a quote from the *Book of Joshua* in the Old Testament, referring to the two spies sent to reconnoitre Jericho ahead of the Hebrew army: "*When you went over the Jordan and came to Jericho, the citizens of Jericho fought against you, and also the Amorites, the Perizzites, the Canaanites, the Hittites, the Girgashites, the Hivites, and the Jebusites; and I handed them over to you. I sent the hornet ahead of you, which drove out before you the two kings of the Amorites; it was not by your sword or by your bow. I gave you a land on which you had not laboured, and towns that you had not built, and you live in them; you eat the fruit of vineyards and olive groves you did not plant.*"

If this hadn't occurred during Holy Mass, Fr Jan Kowalski would have laughed at such a coincidence. Any fiction reader would disbelieve it as grossly artificial in a novel. But in this instance, *God* was the novelist. There they were, the two 'spies' sent by 'Joshua' in preparation for the takeover. And yet, their intentions couldn't have been more peaceful. Furthermore, in the Old Testament the city of Jericho hadn't called the Jews for help — despite Rahab's hospitality to the spies — whereas the Bishop of Hpagok himself had invited them. Out of discretion, though, Fr Kowalski thought of leaving noiselessly before all heads would turn and stare at the two foreigners in long white habits at the back of St Joseph's Church. But no one seemed to have noticed them.

After Holy Mass, the meeting with the parish priest Fr Mark Myat and with the Vicar General Fr Camille Malung went rather well. "St Joseph's was built in 1881 by the priests of the *Missions Etrangères de Paris,*" Fr Mark proudly explained. "You see, the titles of each station of the Cross are written in French. We never got to translate them into Burmese. We maintained St Joseph's well. We even kept the old altar and the altar rail. But our numbers have dropped terribly over the past five years because of the chemical pollution. By now the soil has mostly been decontaminated. But I still only drink bottled water. The Shwekai Borough Council says tap water is fine to drink though. No risk at all of course if used as Holy Water for sprinkling, since Fr Malung said you require a lot of it. Sadly, safe water came back too late. Most inhabitants went away, and our parishioners won't come back now. We just can't afford this church any longer. It will be yours to keep up." Fr Malung noticed that very few Chinese were present at the morning Mass just offered. "I hope you will manage to attract our newcomers, if they really like the old Latin Mass. That's why the Bishop invited you." On hearing that Fr Kowalski wished to offer his private Mass in the late afternoon, Fr Malung expressed his intention to attend. "I watched your Old Mass online twice, but I've never been at one for real."

*   *   *

The gilded scissors barely touched the contorted branches of what looked like a forest of very old but tiny oak trees. They were set on the side of a rocky hill across a vast porcelain tray covered with microscopic moss and peopled with red-clad figurines and small pagodas along which a rivulet ran. A small ancient-looking man with a very thin long moustache was ceremoniously pruning the plants. "My sons, small is beautiful. Cultivating smallness is an art. As Catholics, we call it a virtue. One day, *you* also will master the art of *shuihan penjing*. Please, never allow foreigners to call it *'bonsai.'* We are not Japanese! Remember that we the Ricceans are heirs to twenty centuries of civilisation. Following the example of the illustrious Matteo Ricci, our forefathers laboured to incorporate the tenets of Catholicism into the ancestral Chinese culture. They cultivated unity. O dear unity, sweet unity, decorous unity! When I am gone to my fathers, dear children, please, never allow division into the Church or into our beloved family. Remember that this miniature landscape stands for our little congregation, placed as an *ex voto* before the Blessed Mother of Dong-Lu, that she may keep it united always."

The China Sea filled the background of the vast tiled terrace where, every Saturday after lunch, the venerable old man performed the ritual micro-gardening, surrounded by several dozens of young men wearing, like his, but less ornate, red traditional Chinese robes. Different birds were displayed on the square mandarin badges sown on the chest of each cleric: egrets, pheasants, herons, or swallows. As a poetical and subtle incentive to humility, the symbolic gradation of avian hierarchy as defined in the protocol of the Imperial court of old was reversed in the community. For the Ricceans, the noblest birds marked the lowest rank, and vice versa. Thus, the just-tonsured young seminarians bore fiery phoenixes; right above them in seniority, the Porters bore multicoloured peacocks; Lectors bore silvery cranes, and so on until the senior priests who bore mere magpies. The five Attendant members of the Palatial Council bore robins, barely visible against the red background of their mandarin badges. The Founder was the only one whose chest badge displayed an exquisitely embroidered little sparrow.

Dexterously manipulated in the wrinkled hands of the Founder, the small gilded scissors seemed to float over the tiny oak branches, soothing rather than pruning them, as the fatherly voice explained further: "Through many trials, our little family developed across China and its area of influence and we, the Ricceans, are fortunate to keep alive the palatial spirituality so tastefully displayed by the Chinese emperors of old. The precious badges on our imperial-red robes (after the Ming court ceremonial, you will recall), remind a world oblivious of eternity of the celestial court of which our humble community is honoured to offer a dedicated anticipation, albeit limited. And what of our Empress, dear sons? Here in Macao, we learnt from Our Blessed Mother of Dong-Lu to resist persecution and to spread the reign of her divine Son, our divine Emperor Jesus, with meekness, all over the East. We do not forget Our Lady of Fatima either, who connects us with the Portuguese origin of this peninsula. Her Immaculate Heart will triumph, we believe it. And what, dear sons, is more conducive to reaching this sublime goal than the traditional liturgy of the Mass?" The Founder of the Ricceans had a deep Marian devotion, especially to Our Lady of Dong-Lu. At the foot of her picture on the façade, every Saturday after *shuihan penjing*, his slow and probably painful genuflexion was an edifying sight: both hands held his bamboo walking stick while the five Palatial Attendants supported his elbows.

From the large mansion behind, a dignitary stepped onto the terrace and, bowing before the old man, whispered a confidential message. On hearing the news, the patriarch slowly laid his scissors upon a crimson cushion carried by an acolyte. He then

remained immobile for a nearly half a minute, bowed before the
Marian depiction on the wall above the porcelain tray. None of
the young men behind him dared to move or utter a word, but
all knew that something important was happening. This, their
revered Founder confirmed before peacefully walking back to
the building: "Dear children, please pray for our brethren in
Burma. It may well be that more work will be laid upon their frail
shoulders. Pray that they may generously perform it, should it be
God's holy will and Our Lady's." At that moment, as if approving
of the petition, a dozen scarlet macaws flew off the nearby banyan
trees, a grace-filled firework of red feathers. The old man bowed
again towards the wide mosaic of the Blessed Mother of Dong-Lu
displayed on the neo-baroque facade and, followed by the five
Palatial Attendants, disappeared inside the mansion.

*　*　*

Bishop Pius Thaung was perplexed. Everything had been
arranged for the Hyacinthians to take over St Joseph's at
Shwekai in September, and there was barely one week left
until the beginning of October. But having received further
information from Rome, his vicar general was suggesting more
candidates. All met the requirements of being genuine experts
in the old Latin Mass and were based in Asia, although not
Chinese citizens. Fr Camille Malung described his findings:
"Yes, Your Excellency, time is running out. I know that more
formerly Chinese workers — now Burmese — arrived last month
with their families. I deplore that they have not really shown
interest for the Ordinary Form Masses available to them at
Shwekai. Like you, I had a rather good impression of the Hyacinthian Dominicans, and I agree that it would be awkward to
cancel their appointment at St Joseph's in Shwekai City, even
though it hasn't been made public yet. But in Rangoon last
week I came across the Riccean Fathers. They run a parish
in the nearby diocese of Loikhon and attended the episcopal

consecration of my seminary classmate, now the new auxiliary bishop of Rangoon, as you know. (He was touched by your card and sorry that your health had prevented you from travelling with me.) These Ricceans seem better acquainted with the Asian culture than our Hyacinthians. For instance, they wear traditional Chinese robes and head covers with tassels. Their headquarters are in Macao, which is about as Chinese as one can be outside mainland China. This would make them better accepted by our formerly Chinese workers. More importantly even, the Ricceans offer the Ordinary Form of the Mass in Burmese as well as the Extraordinary Form Mass in Latin."

"Here you must be mistaken, Father. I know little about the Riccean Fathers, but if there is one thing certain about them, it is that they are staunchly set on the old Latin Mass and surely would never think of offering the modern Mass. From the pictures I saw on the magazine they sent me (beautifully produced indeed), their liturgical style is more ornate and flamboyant than the Hyacinthians. All these boyish priests or seminarians wearing red silk, like baby cardinals, make their high Mass look like a mini conclave to me. With such an elaborate display, I would never imagine them supporting the sober liturgy designed after the last Council, even though they might attend it on occasions. I must say that, by contrast, I feel at bit more at home with the simplicity of the Hyacinthians. And if geography matters, well, is not the Hyacinthian Provincial House for Asia in Hong Kong, on Lantau Island, precisely where I wrote to Fr Roman Potocki, their Provincial?"

"I shared Your Excellency's surprise when, in Rangoon at the consecration ceremony last Saturday, I saw two Ricceans vest in the sacristy of the Cathedral. They were undoubtedly putting on the archdiocesan stoles and chasubles, wore no maniples and concelebrated with all of us. I allowed myself to take a picture with my phone in case you wished to see for yourself. A Hyacinthian Father was present as well, only sitting in choir.

I had first mistaken him for a 'modern' Dominican. But that one didn't concelebrate, and knelt instead during Consecration. He received Holy Communion from the new bishop later, kneeling and on the tongue. Puzzled as I was, I chatted with the Riccean Fathers over refreshments, after the celebration. They seemed concerned when hearing about your invitation to the Hyacinthians in Shwekai. 'But the Hyacinthians refuse to offer the New Mass. It is divisive. What about unity?' they asked me. I wasn't sure what to answer."

Having silently examined the pictures on his vicar general's phone, Bishop Pius Thaung stood up from his desk, walked to the window and stared at the rain in the courtyard. He was intrigued and disappointed. In his kind shepherd's heart, he wanted a solution for these six hundred new souls committed to his care and truly thought he had found it in the Hyacinthians. But Fr Malung had a point. Unity was essential. He couldn't push for an agreement with these neo-Dominicans if the Ricceans proved more willing to blend into his diocese. Joseph Stalin's contemptuous remark about the Church's lack of military power came back to his memory: "The Vatican, how many divisions?" Bishop Thaung wished Stalin's assumption had been correct; but he knew that the Church had "divisions," far too many divisions, and they affected her unity.

An objection came to the bishop, however, which he put to his vicar general: "If the Ricceans say the New Mass as well as the Old, it will make them less easily welcomed by our former Chinese refugees. You were the one, Fr Malung, who stressed how inexperienced our new flock is with the Church's liturgical and hierarchical unity. It seems to me that our formerly Chinese minority will trust the Hyacinthians more, precisely because they say only the Old Mass. After decades as underground Catholics, acquainted exclusively with the earlier form of the Roman rite, won't they need every support to feel fully at home in the Church universal?"

Fr Malung seemed to have foreseen the argument. He lay a brochure printed in Chinese and English on his superior's desk: "Your Excellency thinks wisely. Would it not then be even more reassuring for this little group to be assigned priests known for their total absence of 'compromise,' as some would describe it, with Rome and with us diocesan clergy? What about the Sartorians? Although they were originally founded in Italy—the town of Sartori is near Vicenza, I read on their flyer—they have very few missions left in Europe but are big in the Philippines and in India. In 1951, they moved their headquarters to Taiwan, in Taipei. Surely, our new Burmese workers would feel totally at home with these intransigent priests from the 'Republic of China.'"

Bishop Pius Thaung admired his vicar general's finesse. How cleverly, and politely, he unfolded his little strategy! The Sartorians were in an irregular canonical situation. It explained why they didn't show up in the Vatican Directory. But their sacraments were recognised as valid by the Holy See, which had recently extended their faculties to hear confessions. As a bishop, he couldn't approve of their dissidence. There was no such thing as free-lance Catholic clergy. Hadn't they even set up their own tribunals? Who had granted them jurisdiction to annul marriages? And didn't they re-baptise and re-confirm their lay faithful, and even re-ordain priests joining them from the dioceses? No, this was unacceptable. On the other hand, Bishop Pius Thaung couldn't deny a certain interest in this strong and growing community, which had made it its trade mark to maintain the Roman traditions of the Church when, to tell the truth, very few within the Church seemed to care much for such treasures. Could it be that Fr Malung's cunning scheme wasn't as far-fetched as it sounded at first? Had not the Pope granted the Sartorians permission to witness marriages validly, subject to receiving delegation from the local pastor? In that case, could he not, as diocesan Ordinary, appoint a couple of them to take care of his six hundred traditionalist souls?

"Your Excellency, I meant to mention the Missionaries of St Joseph of Saigon, too. I didn't know them but your contact in Rome, Mgr Phang, added that entry to the updated list he emailed me. It seems as if they stand at the milder end of the traditionalist spectrum because they embraced the liturgical reform like everybody. Since the 1970s though, their numbers were shrinking and, having tried the Extraordinary Form, they experienced a rather spectacular surge of vocations over the past ten years. Perhaps they..."

The attention of Bishop Pius Thaung was suddenly caught by "*Chairman Meow*," his Burmese cat, who jumped onto his master's mahogany desk. Bishop Thaung was very fond of his pet's silky coat and deep blue eyes. He also found the contrasting white "gloves" or "socks" on each paw very handsome. Fr Malung left his sentence unfinished, guessing that the bishop had received more information than he was able to assimilate for the present. It was wiser, the vicar general gauged, to let these many new options settle in the mind of his superior and discuss them again later.

"Look what you've done, naughty *Chairman*, pushing the brochures down on the carpet. I know what you want, little scoundrel. Come with me to the kitchen. Thank you very much Fr Malung, I will think about all this and make a decision soon. This way, *Meow*." Bishop Thaung took the feline in his arms as it was about soya milk time for the pet. As for him, he would enjoy a cup of tea while pondering this modern sequel to the eighteenth-century "Chinese Rites controversy," as it appeared to him.

*　*　*

Fr Jan Kowalski was feeling weary as he got out of the car in front of Bishop's House. It had been another very long drive from Mandalay, this time to Hpagok where Bishop Pius Thaung had his residence. Thankfully, the rainy season had ended, making the trip safer and quicker. It was 4pm that Saturday, 28th

September 2019 and Fr Kowalski had just finished reciting First Vespers of the feast of St Michael the Archangel as the car entered the town: "Happy feast day, Fr Michal, in anticipation!" At the wheel sat now *Fr* Michal Symanski, who had just been ordained a priest by a Cardinal from Rome. Would this concrete mark of support from the highest authorities dispose the Bishop of Hpagok in their favour? While this second meeting, this time booked with His Lordship, bode well, nothing was signed as yet and Fr Kowalski had been tipped off by his confrere in Rangoon who had seen "Riccean priests in animated conversation with Fr Malung at the Cathedral." Opportunities for traditional orders to open new places of apostolate were still rare. That made it challenging sometimes to keep a healthy balance between the good of one's community and abandonment to divine Providence. Would they ever offer the Holy Sacrifice of the Mass at St Joseph's in Shwekai, on that high altar ideally designed for the traditional liturgy? The date envisaged for the inauguration had been postponed once, and was now prudently left open.

On their way to Hpagok, time and again Fr Kowalski had examined the options with his young confrere. In between two rosaries, they had come to the same conclusion: that honesty was the best strategy. Not that the Hyacinthian Dominicans could ever envisage a different one. Had they not been founded specifically to spread and teach the Catholic truth? To them, the traditional liturgy was the tool best suited to their end as preachers. They could envisage no exception, because the dogmatic truths about the Incarnation, the Redemption, the most holy Mother of God, the sacraments and more did not change, and were best expressed through the traditional form of the Roman rite. In their opinion, this principle applied in every circumstance, to give glory to God and enlighten souls.

The Hyacinthian Provincial in Hong Kong had been reassuring over the phone: "Speak plainly to the Bishop. If Our Lady

wants us in Shwekai, she will tell him." Young Fr Symanski
had nodded at this, adding: "Yes, let us be completely *Wysiwyg*
with him."

Perplexed, Fr Kowalski had enquired: "Sorry? What do you
mean by '*wiz-ee-wig*'? That isn't Polish, is it?"

"Of course not. WYSIWYG is an acronym for '*what you see
is what you get*' in computer programming. It means 'no dis-
tortion': what you see on your screen is exactly what will come
out once printed. Without it, size, spaces and colours, fonts and
layout are often altered unintentionally."

"I see. Well, I'm glad *you* are in charge of our website, rather
than I. Now let's get out of your fancy rental car and speak plain
Wysiwyg to His Lordship; and may St Hyacinth inspire us all."

Standing in their white Dominican habits on the steps outside Bishop's House, the two religious were met by an unexpected feline butler. "*Chairman Meow*, stay in, it's too wet for
you outside." But with a welcoming purr the pet was already
rubbing its back against the legs of Fr Symanski. "Please take it
away, Father, I'm allergic to cats!" the unfortunate friar begged
of his confrere in Polish while starting to sneeze noisily. Thankfully the animal leaped into the arms of the Bishop who greeted
his visitors and let them in.

Well into the discussion about the takeover of St Joseph's
Church at Shwekai, Bishop Pius Thaung asked how the Hyacinthians could assist, should the need arise, and help out in
neighbouring parishes. Fr Kowalski assured him of their avail-
ability for teaching catechism and instructing converts, baptising,
hearing confessions, anointing the sick and burying the dead,
or for any other pastoral involvement, including of course the
Holy Sacrifice of the Mass. On this, Fr Malung took the liberty
of asking whether they would use the Ordinary Form missal to
cover for diocesan priests. Fr Kowalski replied that their charism
was intrinsically connected with the traditional Dominican rite
and that they were obliged to help accordingly. An embarrassing

silence was interrupted, thankfully, by the assertive vocalizations of "*Chairman Meow*" clawing at the side door as if milk time had come again. Bishop Thaung delegated to Fr Malung the essential task of feeding the cat. Poor Fr Symanski, still sneezing, was relieved to see the pet leave the room.

From the open door of the nearby kitchen, the vicar general missed the Bishop's next question. But he could now hear the following quotation being read by Fr Kowalski: "*Several forms of the Latin rite have always existed, and were only slowly withdrawn, as a result of the coming together of the different parts of Europe. Before the Council there existed side by side with the Roman rite, the Ambrosian rite, the Mozarabic rite of Toledo, the rite of Braga, the Carthusian rite, the Carmelite rite, and best known of all, the Dominican rite, and perhaps still other rites of which I am not aware. No one was ever scandalized that the Dominicans, often present in our parishes, did not celebrate like diocesan priests but had their own rite. We did not have any doubt that their rite was as Catholic as the Roman rite, and we were proud of the richness inherent in these various traditions.*"

Fr Malung walked back into the office on time to catch the Bishop's reply: "Was the Holy Father himself making this point, Fr Kowalski?"

"No, Your Excellency. He was then speaking only as Cardinal Joseph Ratzinger, at the conference for the tenth anniversary of the motu proprio *Ecclesia Dei* in Rome. That was in October 1998 and I heard him with my own ears, being present then as a young friar in formation. Since then, over two hundred diocesan bishops — several of them cardinals — have entrusted a ministry to us."

"But Your Excellency," Fr Malung ventured, "these six hundred formerly Chinese people surely never attended Mass in a traditional *Dominican* parish. Would they not be completely lost if this Dominican rite, rather than the old *Roman* rite, were the one made available to them? I ask this without personal grievances, Fr Kowalski. I attended your private Mass last time at St Joseph's and I found it interesting."

"With respect, Fr Malung," Fr Kowalski explained, "compared with the modern Mass, the traditional Dominican rite is a mere variation on the traditional Roman one. Your former underground Catholics would have no difficulty at all identifying every gesture performed by our priests at the altar and spontaneously responding: '*Et cum spiritu tuo.*' They would feel completely at home."

Bishop Pius Thaung watched the Hyundai SUV go down the driveway, turn left onto the main road and disappear toward Shwekai where the two Hyacinthians would spend the night. He was glad to have eventually reached a satisfactory solution. Of course, he had observed how the younger friar kept his distance with "*Chairman Meow.*" But could that *really* be held against them?

VIII
Dom Manuel's Funeral
(2019, BRAZIL)

O SENHOR É O MEU PASTOR; NADA ME FAL-tará. Walking along the corridor tiled with tree-patterned *azulejos* of bright colours, Domitila kept humming the chorus of the hymn rehearsed with the community that morning. "Yes, *The Lord is my shepherd, I shall not want.* And yet," she smiled as she knocked at the thick eucalyptus doors, "do we not call João our 'Shepherd' as well? We ask for his advice in public matters such as the running of the community, but also private, like ... —like this very sorry business of poor Padre Carlos."

"Domitila, do come in, Sister." The serene face of a fatherly man in his early sixties — slightly younger than her — had appeared in the open doorway. She liked his long beard; like Moses. He spoke in a low voice, so as not to awake the sleeping infant in his arms.

"This is Oscar, my twenty-seventh grandchild. I'm babysitting for my daughter-in-law Agnieszka; you know, the Catholic one", Shepherd João Hirt whispered, leading Domitila toward the prayer corner of the vast room, formerly the Chapter Room of Leão Abbey (or Maristela, as was its religious title). The thick carpet was a welcome addition to the old Chapter Room, like a shroud of comfort spread over the austere origins of the Cistercian building. The monks were gone. The last ones had left about a year earlier and the diocese had asked the Novárvore Community to turn the abbey into a spirituality centre. A real bonus, the current Shepherd was an Evangelical Christian. Interdenominational bookings had been immediate and the future of Maristela was secured.

Shepherd João invited Domitila to one of the handmade prayer benches, smiling: "I used to sit cross-legged for a full hour. Not anymore, since I got bursitis in my hip joint. This stool changed my life: it keeps my spine straight as it puts no strain on the back during meditation." Domitila thought to herself that putting the infant in the cradle would be even better for his back. The large ecumenical Bible opened before them was a gift left by the monks. They had used it for years.

"Where did you say they found him? In the tower?"

It had taken Domitila ten minutes to explain the painful story to Shepherd João. Padre Carlos had been the priest at the parish of Domitila's daughter, Isabel. Three days earlier, he'd hanged himself in the church steeple. Apparently, he'd attempted to kiss a nineteen-year-old girl whom he was preparing for the sacraments. She wasn't traumatised at all, but her mother had harassed the priest for months, calling him a predator to his face every time she stood before him at Mass to receive the Bread from his hand. The local newspaper had quoted the Bishop saying that Padre Carlos was very popular with youngsters, adding: "It's a real challenge when one realises that one fails to reach one's potential." Isabel and her husband Deodoro were obviously devastated. Padre Carlos had become their friend, visiting them often for meals and training their children to serve at Eucharistic celebrations.

Walking back to her cell, Domitila pondered the question posed by Shepherd João. Celibacy was the problem, she'd suggested. He'd answered that as a Protestant he respected the Catholic custom for priests not to marry, even though he was grateful for his years of happiness until his wife's death, and for his large family. Then he'd asked *what* mattered most in the life of Padre Carlos. Domitila wasn't sure. Being with people? Running the parish? Leading pilgrimages? Yes, he had liked pilgrimages, especially to the national shrine of Aparecida, less than two hours away. Shepherd João had said that people often go off the rails when their core identity is not recognised or valued by those who love them.

Sitting by her bed, Domitila gazed at the icon of Rublev's Trinity without seeing it. Instead, the image of her brother Adalberto crossed her mind. No, it wasn't the same at all. Adalberto had been dispensed from his vows, like thousands of priests in the 1970s. He was happily married with the blessing of the Church. And yet, was there anything she could—should—have done at the time to support him in his priestly calling? On the other hand, why bother, or why interfere? Was it not best for anyone to follow their path to happiness, even though it took unexpected turns? If Adalberto had not left the priesthood, he might well have been a gloomy cleric, ending up like Padre Carlos. Or worse—if that were possible, like those two priests she'd read about in the Rio papers three months earlier, who'd been sentenced to nearly a year in prison for accessing child porn websites.

Speaking of which, Domitila had appreciated the frankness of Shepherd João regarding their own sad case. Loide was a deacon from Mozambique. He'd joined the Novárvore Community as a teenager and had trained in Brazil. After Christmas, it was found that he had been grossly imprudent with an under-age teenage girl of the Community (with several of them, in fact). He'd been sent back to Africa. Thankfully, prosecution had been avoided. But Shepherd João had insisted on a full disclosure to the Novárvore members and had invited all to stricter, more prudent rules (Domitila was loath to read the thick "safeguarding document"). She had met Loide only a couple of times and knew very little of him, apart from his skills as a guitarist. Still, now looking at the Rublev icon by her bed, she wondered if there was anything she could have done to accompany this young brother deacon on his consecrated path. What was his core identity? What made him happiest? Playing the guitar? In truth, she preferred the piano.

* * *

A motorbike passed Domitila by as she entered the wood. She stopped and waited for the roaring to fade away until the sounds of birds and rustling branches could be heard again. Up there, on the left, this white-bearded manakin reminded her of . . . Dear Shepherd João . . . He'd been insistent in wanting to drive her home. But she'd felt like walking the two miles or so, to lower her carbon footprint — and her weight. She also wanted more time to think. So much had happened since Afonso's fall ten months earlier and his semi-vegetative state since. She'd had all the time to prepare for it during his slow decline over the past couple of decades. He was still with her now, she knew. They'd had a beautiful life as a couple. Together they'd overcome prejudice ("That nurse, marrying the eldest son of the Arval estate!"); disability (Afonso's multiple sclerosis, diagnosed in his early twenties, hadn't prevented her from keeping him walking until he was 72); disfavour (Dom Manuel, Afonso's father, would get the tombstone he deserved, just wait and see).

As she came out of the wood she saw it in the distance, nestled amidst shallow hills — the *fazenda*. *Fazenda* Arval was one of the oldest original coffee plantations in Vale do Paraiba, the Brazilian equivalent of the county of Kent in England: "Where it all began." The Arval family had long ago shifted from coffee to horses. "We're horse people, and have been for generations." That's how Dom Manuel had introduced the family to Domitila once it was confirmed that she would become more than a nurse to his eldest son Afonso. She still resented the ongoing hypocrisy of her father-in-law. Her crippled husband could obviously not ride. Was it why the patriarch seemed to despise Afonso so much? But their son Rafael, Dom Manuel's grandson, was an accomplished Lusitano rider. Yet, instead of supporting his grandchild and main heir, the old man had favoured his younger grandson Luiz instead, a vulgar motorbike collector! So much for the importance of riding horses! That Luiz nephew of hers had been a real pain from his teenage years. He used to vroom around the stables on his silly Kawasaki, frightening the stallions as if on purpose during Rafael's jumping exercises. Through his favouritism, Dom Manuel was the one who had caused rivalry between the two cousins and eventually led her son, her Rafael, to where he now was.

"Rafael! Oh, that he might come *alone* to the ceremony!" Domitila moaned. She could not face the prospect of Rafael's friend "*Guiomar*" standing behind him by the family tomb, with everyone watching. "With a samba dancer! My God, how on earth did my son fall that low? After so promising a beginning. And it's now nearly one year since the pair moved together into that flat in Rio. Will I have no grandchildren, I mean, none bearing the name of Arval, despite Isabel expecting her third one? Will I spend the rest of my life alone with an unconscious husband in this mansion of ours?"

She took a deep breath, looked at the great house in the distance, tightened her fists around the straps of her pink rucksack, and started walking fast down the slope. After all, she was barely sixty-nine and could even run if she felt like it. So she did, slowing down after two minutes. Excellent, that had done her good. "At least," she remembered, "Luiz won't attend. It's a consolation." Domitila wasn't sure why her nephew had declined her offer to bless his grandfather's tombstone. What was the use of having a priest among one's close relatives if he was not willing to bless the family vault with his grandfather's tomb completed at long last? Perhaps he should have remained a motorbike collector instead.

*   *   *

They had all come, or nearly. How impressively the Arval family tree had grown; the birth of its one-hundred-and-first member being expected around Pentecost. With Dom Manuel resting under his finely chiselled new slab and Afonso comatose, Domitila had felt slightly awkward as the *de facto* head of the clan. It hadn't looked that way when she'd married the just-turned-forty crippled Arval heir, thirty-eight years earlier. She'd amply proven her dedication to him, to the family, to the estate and to the Church. What more could they have expected?

Padre Roque, appointed parish priest at the nearby town now a year earlier, had blessed the slab, praising its beautiful design. Domitila had not tried to hide the sense of peace or relief she'd experienced when reading the simple words: "Dom Manuel Arval, 23 January 1920 — 18 March 2018, R. I. P." She had insisted on gilded characters. During lunch after the short ceremony, there had been the odd bitter comment from Beatriz of course, Luiz's mother: "It's great you could make it today Tila: we missed you last month for the First Anniversary Mass." She couldn't help it, poor Beatriz. Her motherly pride for Luiz made her incapable of showing gratitude. She knew full well that Domitila had emailed Luiz, offering to pay his airfare if he could fly here again for the stone-laying ceremony. Was it her fault if the sculptor's sickness had delayed the event by nearly two months?

As to Dom Manuel's First Anniversary Mass, she admitted to herself that it had been unfortunate. The date had clashed with the unofficial selection runs in preparation for the Grande Prêmio São Paulo. What was she to do? With Afonso totally incapacitated for the first time, who, if not the director's wife, would represent Stud Arval at so crucial a turf event? Henrique couldn't go alone, being only the manager. She had been right to attend. *Rio Piedra* had run superbly and was now among the top-five favourites for the Grande Prêmio on 5th May following. The Stud could surely do with a victory, but even a second or third would help tremendously. It would crush these rumours of decline, as if Dom Manuel had been necessary for Stud Arval to breed great runners. Why, the old despot hadn't attended a race for years anyway!

That evening, Domitila walked alone across the vast rooms of the empty mansion. She'd been trying to pray, with little success. The children had declined her offer to stay the night. Rafael was back in Rio — to his *"Guiomar"* — and Isabel had to get her house ready for some friends visiting. Two children, gone. What a contrast with the tribes of her brothers- and sisters-in-law. Each of them had between three and seven children and many grandchildren. On the contrary, she was glad *not* to have followed the path of Afonso's parents — six girls and five boys! Not a surprise, coming from Dom Manuel. That wasn't a life, at least for a wife. Thank God, science had improved all that. In modern Brazil, a dedicated Christian woman like her was able to invest her energy in urgent social causes (she sponsored a shelter for addicts on the outskirts of the estate), in addition to the care of her husband. Remembering that it was the carer's afternoon off, Domitila walked up the monumental staircase and entered Afonso's room on tiptoe. He seemed asleep. She whispered to him as had been her habit since the beginning of his semi-coma, hoping he understood:

"It all went well, darling. Your dad is at rest under a very fine marble slab. Luiz was the only one missing. He'd emailed me that it was too difficult for him to fly back after having been here last month for the anniversary Mass. I can't see why. I'd found affordable direct flights from Luanda to São Paulo. He said that in his part of Angola, by the Ocean, the situation is tense, so he was advised to remain with his flock. Well, we would hear it on the news if conflicts had started again over there, wouldn't we? Do you think he's still upset because . . . of last year's funeral? Dom Manuel's funeral . . . Here we go again."

Letting his hand go from hers, she walked to the tall window. The sun had long set but the night was bright. A couple of equine silhouettes showed in the paddock on the right, immobile. Were the horses asleep? Not long ago she had realised that these fascinating animals can sleep even with their eyes open. Imagine that . . . In the distance, she could see the darker line of the woods against the paler sky. A cluster of electric lights betrayed the little town of Leão. She wondered if she could catch a glimpse of the steeple of Maristela church right behind the trees. Was Shepherd João asleep? Or playing with his grandchildren? No, the little ones would be in bed, surely. Wishing she could soon do the same, she remembered to check if Greta was back indoors. She liked to have their Canary Mastiff with them at night (she was a rather harmless *presa* which "protected their domestic environment").

Back downstairs, Domitila refilled with water Greta's bowl in the kitchen. The temperature was still high for the season: 22.1°C. Searching the ground floor, she soon found the pet lying in the Equestrian Room. She crouched and stroked the dog, wondering why Greta fancied that particular place in the mansion. She for one would not have liked to sleep under the stuffed head of *Introibo*, the legendary thoroughbred of Arval. She and Afonso had turned this room into a museum celebrating the runner's memorable victories. The very saddle it wore at the 1998 Grande Prêmio now sat on a life size Plexiglas replica of the horse's body, with its actual stuffed head fitted at the end and its tail at the other. The impression was rather powerful, but would not have been conducive to a restful night, she reckoned, if her bed had been set down in that room.

*　*　*

This time Shepherd João had met her under the pergola, on the lawn behind the former abbey. Although one could be seen from the house, it was private enough to discuss further her personal matters. The Shepherd had no grandchildren with him that afternoon. Was it why he hadn't seen her in his study like the day before, Domitila suddenly wondered? Was he applying the tighter safeguarding rules even to his relationship with her? She wasn't sure why she felt such a hypothesis at once disconcerting and flattering. Come on, surely, they were both long past flirting age. Still ... After Shepherd João had walked back inside, with his calm and light pace, she was shocked to discover in her heart a longing for this spiritual man which, in brutal honesty, could involve more than her soul. Never once had she been aware of such an inclination toward him, she reckoned. So, was she being romantic at nearly sixty-nine? Please, no.

This was not, thank God, what she had just discussed with him. As usual, he had let her do most of the talking. He was such a good listener. The knot of emotions and frustrations in her heart felt gradually disentangled as she shared with him her exasperations, her regrets and her hopes. He had thought it nice of her to listen to *Radio Ecclesia* a year earlier. After decades of oppression, the Angolan government had finally allowed Catholic radio broadcast in early 2018 and Fr Luiz had been invited to speak about the Latin Mass. He'd emailed his family the time in case they wished to hear him live. Domitila had made the effort of tuning in (at 5:45am with the time zone difference), and had emailed back a brief compliment after his forty-minute presentation. What she hadn't said was that his talk had only confirmed her impression of ecclesial estrangement between her nephew and her. Seriously, did Angolan Christians under totalitarian rule really need to know that "horse hair made great holy water brush sprinklers"! Why draw their attention to this? Was that the core Gospel to the poor of the earth, the twenty-first century kerygma, the living Good News to touch the hearts of those in dire need? Put simply, Domitila felt that Luiz didn't belong to the same Church as her any more.

Shepherd João smiled a little at this admission that Church affiliation mattered to her, in this case. Domitila wished she had expressed herself more tactfully before him, an Evangelical Protestant. This new Luiz, she explained, seemed to see everything in terms of dogmas, sacrifices and traditions, while she sought social awareness, fraternal assistance and inspiration. Up to the early 2000s he had been an infuriating motorbike collector and biker admittedly, but somehow normal as a teenager. At least there were no drugs involved, and if girls were, he kept it discreet. His parents and siblings, as well as Afonso and she and his other uncles and aunts could still identify his main interest—motorcycling—even though not sharing it. The change must have started during that motorbike trip with these two friends of his in 2001—the same winter when Rafael had passed his *vestibular* to start his Law degree at USP. Luiz had casually mentioned staying a couple of nights on the way at some religious house near Nova Friburgo. No one paid much attention until the boy went back there to spend an entire week—with no bikers around. His parents were deeply concerned on discovering that the place was Holy Cross Monastery, an "integrist" community.

Domitila paused, wondering whether Shepherd João was *au fait* with the spectrum of dissident trends around Roman Catholicism. Surprisingly, he nodded: "Some say the Tridentine Mass without permission from the Pope, and others do it with his permission, isn't that right?" She wasn't sure that things were as simple as that. The Tridentine Mass was the issue, regardless of the level of tolerance granted. Yes, she went on, the family was relieved when Luiz denied any intention of becoming a monk in Nova Friburgo. But a year later came the shattering news. He'd joined a newly formed priestly community near Rio de Janeiro. Officially they had Rome's blessing, but who could ignore that they were a reactionary and extremist lot? Some of them were even in contact with the *TFP*.

Shepherd João enquired what the TFP was. Domitila explained, as she had been warned in the diocesan magazine, that the TFP—aka *Tradition, Family, Property*—"used their wealth to impose the social reign of Christ upon society against freedom of religion." In a gesture of meditation familiar to him, the Shepherd applied the tips of his joined fingers to his lips. After some reflection, he said that he would like to learn more about them. Although money was not the safest means, he conceded, the goal sounded evangelical enough to him. "Should we not all try to build and extend the kingdom of Christ?" Domitila realised that Shepherd João's background as a Protestant made him less aware of the dangers of proselytising. For all his wisdom, he was less informed of the duty to contain one's faith within private boundaries. Should she shift the conversation to another topic? With all due ecumenical respect, she could not condone religious exhibitionism or imposition on fellow citizens. That was a non-negotiable Catholic feature.

* * *

The Rublev icon would not answer her questions. Sitting on her feet in her little cell, by her bed on the narrow carpet, Domitila prayed earnestly. Why, dear God, was the relationship so difficult with several of her in-laws? She had tried and tried again, with some temporary successes and many failures. This funeral slab-laying ceremony the day before had revived many tensions from the past. They agreed on fundamentals. For instance, none of her many Arval relatives attended the Latin Mass. They were content with Catholic worship. Some nephews had been involved with Rafael in setting up *Alpha Course* groups and her sister-in-law's daughter managed the shelter for addicts on the estate, also with Rafael's support. They praised her involvement with the Bishop in training lay ministers of funerals. At the family council meeting two years previously, they had supported almost unanimously Afonso's suggestion of inviting the Novárvore Community to take over Maristela Abbey (the Arvals were one of the four *fazendas* on the ecclesiastical board of the abbey, whose land they had offered in trust a century ago). Only poor Beatriz had objected, of course. Having married into the Leão clan, she was trying to retain an exclusively Catholic presence at the abbey whose name she had come to bear. Her bias was increased as the proud mother of "Fr Luiz Leão." Domitila smiled mockingly as she recalled her sister-in-law's dismay when she exclaimed: "But Luiz offered his First Mass at Leão Abbey. How could we let this church be used in the future for Protestant worship!" A favourable decision had been reached on the condition that the chapel should remain officially under the diocese, and that each of the four families should be allocated permanently a cell at Maristela, hence Domitila's.

Her ankles started hurting from her sitting on her feet. Domitila carefully stood up and reclined on her bed before tingling should start in her legs. "Holy Spirit, you know I'm sincere. Show me if the problem is mere jealousy between Beatriz and me. Is it a clash of mums? How can it be fixed? I've tried everything. But she failed even to mention the significant present of the motorcycle." Yes, that incident had been the last straw. Sometime after Dom Manuel's funeral, Luiz had posted on the family *Whatsapp* group that his motorbike had been stolen three weeks earlier, in Angola. There was a picture of him saying Mass in a dusty village street on a makeshift altar apparently unfolded at the back of his large motorcycle, now lost. Of course, he was turning his back on the camera, as if making a point to ignore the congregation whose young black heads (some veiled!) could be seen in the foreground. Domitila remembered her frustration at seeing the face of her nephew partially reflected in the small side mirror of the motorbike, while on his back hung this awkward rigid piece of vestment, rectangular like a sandwich man board, advertising what? — a flowery cross!

Anyhow, Luiz had urged his relatives *not* to buy another bike for him, because that was just what locals expected of foreign missionaries, he explained, and it would not lead the thief to repentance (his fellow-priest suspected the elder brother of an altar server). Rather, he had been going on foot since then, or cycling to the outposts to visit his flock. But Beatriz had complained in front of Domitila that this situation could not continue as it hindered her son's ministry and put him in danger. So, to make a long story short, in agreement with Afonso, Domitila had purchased online from a retailer in Luanda a robust second hand cross country Yamaha "with Akrapovic titanium pipes" (she remembered that name because it sounded very similar to that of her favourite tennis player, the handsome victor of Flushing Meadows last — a bearded Croatian). The gift bike was more powerful than the one stolen and had been delivered to Luiz's presbytery as a surprise, with a note from her. He had emailed her and his uncle profuse thanks; but Beatriz never once mentioned the gift to them! Had she done even half of this for *their* son? When Rafael quit his Law practice and needed a place in Rio for the homeless he was supporting, did Beatriz raise one little finger to ask her in-laws for solutions? They knew well two local parishes and could easily have found an empty hall, even temporarily.

*   *   *

First! *Rio Piedra* had just won the Grande Prêmio. It would have been a dead heat with *Punic Picnic* (the runner owned by Tunisian media tycoon Tarek Ben Immar) unless a photo finish had vindicated the Arval favourite. Sitting at the rear of the car on her return to the *fazenda*, Domitila felt as if she were on a cloud. After a while she closed her eyes, seemingly sleeping while her youngest brother-in-law Henrique, the Stud manager, continued the animated conversation with the jockey. Money mattered, of course, she knew too well, to keep this large estate going. But it was also a personal victory for the new regime, that is, the post-Dom Manuel era of the Arval clan of which she was, like it or not, the embodiment. Later in the evening, lying in his bed in the large room, Afonso had seemed to understand what the picture of the finish was about as she put it before his eyes. His faint smile was barely perceptible under his two-week-old beard. She left the phone ringing on the mahogany desk behind them, telling her husband it was surely some further enthusiastic relatives and friends expressing their congratulations (even Beatriz and José had texted theirs). When her own phone vibrated in her pocket, reading Rafael's name on the screen, Domitila left the room to speak more easily with her son, not knowing yet that so glorious a day would end in such a way. What a catastrophe! She slept little that night.

The following morning, Shepherd João arrived promptly with his assistant. He'd been at the *fazenda* before, on rare social occasions. He preferred to keep a professional distance, seemingly, and only met with Domitila when she visited Maristela, at least once a week. Finding her in the family mausoleum, as she had said, he left his young Brother Secretary outside, visible through the door left ajar. Domitila was glad of that opportunity to show her Shepherd the fine carved slab laid on Dom Manuel's tomb the previous month. He complimented her on it, and improvised a prayer to the Holy Ghost, asking divine blessings upon the entire Arval family tree. They sat on the marble bench against the back wall of the small chapel. It was refreshingly cool inside and they kept silent for a while. She wasn't sure how to share the news with him. How do you explain to a Christian friend that your only son's partner is having a gender reassignment and will probably "marry" him? Over the phone the night before, Raphael had condoned the sexual confusion of "*Guiomar*," calling it "gender fluidity." He'd spoken very calmly all along. But their conversation had lasted longer than it should have and touched upon very hurtful issues.

Domitila reviewed, this time with Shepherd João, the pros and cons she had been weighing during most of the past night. Her son still believed in God, and even still attended Mass. But if he attempted a civil union with "*Guiomar*," a transgender apparently, even Bishop Joaquim would not ordain him as a permanent deacon. "Deacon Rafael Arval"... Had Domitila given up on that old dream of hers? She thought she had, honestly, years ago. Only, the sudden news of a definitive impediment looming ahead seemed to have resurrected her fancy. It had started some twenty years earlier she guessed, when Joaquim, a seminary comrade of her brother Adalberto, had been made Auxiliary Bishop in São Paulo. Mentioning in a

conversation the need for many more permanent deacons, he
had asked her if Rafael had ever thought of it to her knowledge.
She remembered the illumination this question had caused
in her soul. Yes, her devout son could become a cleric and
still get married, have children and succeed she and her husband as head of the Arval estate. What a huge amount of good
would result from it! How had she never thought of this before?
Afonso had shared her enthusiasm, with the *caveat* that, for all
his devotion in the *Alpha Course* and his service to the addicts,
at the time Rafael had never expressed an attraction to the
permanent diaconate before him. Afonso had even wondered,
to be fair, if it was not sufficient for him to help with parish
governance as a layman, while remaining totally free to run the
estate in the future. But she had thought this was not enough.
What: when the Church was in need of ordained ministers,
when the Church was *calling*, could they, the Arvals, not give
their son to serve the Lord and souls? Was not the Church
calling? Could Afonso not hear?

Shepherd João gently enquired why she'd never mentioned
to him this wish for her son. Well, as she'd said, on seeing
that Rafael gave so vague a response, and once he'd started
practising Law, she had thought her expectation would not
be fulfilled. Sure, when he'd quit Law for charitable work with
the addicts, her hopes had risen again a little, but not much,
because this coincided with his new friendship with "*Guiomar.*"
The Shepherd asked whether her desire to see her son become a
deacon could have been prompted by her nephew's unexpected
vocation to the priesthood. Domitila regretted the vehemence
of her denial—not so much because it was slightly rude to her
sympathising guest, as because it proved his guess true, to some
extent: "Absolutely not! When Bishop Joaquim asked me about
Rafael, Luiz was nowhere near becoming a seminarian. He was
but a biker, a mere biker, a stupid biker!" Once the echo of
her shout along the marble vault of the family mausoleum had

died down, everything was quiet again; until Domitila burst into tears. After a few minutes, Shepherd João stood up and said: "Now Sister, will you show me *Rio Piedra*, the already famous victor of the Grande Prêmio? I watched his spectacular finishing kick on the news yesterday night."

Such a victory had left Domitila little time over the following week. There were interviews to be granted, pictures with *Rio Piedra*, many bookings from all over Brazil (and even from abroad) for groups to visit the estate, not only turf professionals but also school children. She gave thanks to God for such busyness, a welcome diversion to the wound in her heart caused by her son's news and, more subtly and no less painfully, by the gradual realisation that her wishes for Rafael's vocation had perhaps not been fully disinterested.

Watching the sun set one evening, sometime after 5pm, she relished the quiet of nightfall while finding comfort in the presence of Greta, a gigantic body of trusting tenderness at her feet by the garden bench. She nearly felt like asking the dog the burning question: "What do *you* think Greta? Suppose for one moment you were human. Would you have done differently from us, you know... for Dom Manuel's funeral?" Greta gave a perplexed look and Domitila agreed: it *was* complicated.

*   *   *

"I know *Dia das Mães* falls this Sunday, Mum. Yes, of course I think Mother's Day is important. The children will still celebrate it here at home, I mean, with me. You're absolutely right: we *had* planned to come and stay with Father and you at Arval... Yes, with Deodoro and with your grandchildren... Certainly I can still travel. It's only two hours by car and I'm only due in July... Why cancel then? Well, I just feel tired. Nothing more? No, nothing more. Promise. It's only postponed, we'll come on Ascension Day instead at the end of the month... What was that? Padre Carlos' funeral — well, I couldn't attend... I am fine and so is Deodoro. We just need a little more time on our own, you see, as a family unit. Since you're asking, yes, I do see the psychiatrist you recommended ... Dr Bruxoa indeed. Why do you need to know? That is ... Once a week. Frankly, I'm not sure it's worth my time and money... It's not quite the usual psychobabble, but he still suggests weird connections between things that have nothing in common ... What again? Now Mum, perhaps I will keep *this* to myself. Yes, it *is* quite personal, you understand ... I know you only mean to help. I know you wish you could share the burden with me. Sure ... I love you. Congratulations again on *Rio Piedra's* victory. Quite unexpected ... No, you're right, not *that* unexpected. Oh, by the way, I meant to ask you: does Greta still sleep in ... in the Equestrian Room?"

Domitila's heart sank on putting her phone down, by the kitchen window. The prospect of having the grandchildren come and spend the weekend — with Isabel and Deodoro — had made her so happy. They would have eaten on the little table by Afonso's bed. Not the full meal, only the Mothers' Day cake, so as not to tire her husband, poor soul. Domitila put the kettle on again, as the water had stopped boiling during the phone call and she liked it piping hot. And now, Isabel was showing herself difficult. More than difficult, pointed rather. Yes, she'd actually said: "Expecting a third child is quite tiring Mum, believe me." Her implication was clear. She meant that Domitila had no right to insist on her travelling to Arval in her condition, because she'd only ever carried *two* children, not three. What was the matter with Isabel? Obviously, yes, the shock of Padre Carlos' suicide, and the repercussion on the children who knew him well. Perhaps she felt guilty. Yes, guilt was a usual reaction. But what could she have done, poor thing, to prevent the tragedy? Nobody had any idea the man was in such an extreme state. Or else, was Isabel reacting poorly to Dr Bruxoa's therapy? A saddle, he'd said. And he'd asked her about the Equestrian Room. What did that have to do with losing her parish priest?

No, Domitila wouldn't allow that man to stuff her daughter's head with preposterous suggestions!

The whistling kettle was a comforting sound. Domitila waited just a little, pensively, before pouring water in her cup. Ignoring the *Café Arval* box, she picked a tea bag instead. She found hot tea paradoxically refreshing in such heat. But for the dog, *cold* water from the tap, of course. There, a bowl filled to the brim — the third time this afternoon. "Greta!" Not hearing the familiar sound of paws on the wooden floor, Domitila left her cup on the window sill to cool and walked to find where the pet lay. She did not expect to see the mastiff on the main corridor but, surprisingly, the Equestrian Room was also empty, apart from the conspicuous horse. No dog, see? That proved the silliness of that psychotherapist's assumption. The man was simply deranged, yes. Who had recommended him to her again? Domitila lifted up her head, looking *Introibo* straight in the eyes — glass eyes, as it happened. The taxidermist had truly done a superb job, hadn't he? The stuffed head of the stallion was so well preserved that one nearly expected it to neigh, if its neck and body hadn't been made of Plexiglas (the tail was genuine though, and one couldn't tell that some hair was missing). Domitila stroked the smooth leather of the saddle, the one of the Grande Prêmio victory (that is, *one of* the Arval victories, since there had been more since), smiling ironically.

"How absurd. How surreal. So, apparently, I 'saddled my father-in-law'! How much does Dr Bruxoa charge per hour for such tales? In no time would I expose his fables, if he ever inquired of me. First of all, the Equestrian Room was Afonso's idea as much as mine. Second, this room had only been Dom Manuel's for the last two years of his life. When he could not walk alone any longer, rather than remain in his master's suite upstairs, he'd decreed his intention to migrate down to the ground floor 'so as to still be among the living.' (Rather, he meant to exert control for as long he could.) If anything, Afonso and I had tried to dissuade him from turning the sewing room into a nursing care unit. It was all very impractical to have him down here. One had to walk on tiptoes along the corridor to avoid waking him up, even though he claimed that he enjoyed hearing the sounds of everyday life. The tiny bathroom he'd managed to have fitted in the closet by the window was totally unsuitable to bathe a bed-ridden elderly man. And third..."

The sudden visualisation of her dying father-in-law seemed to have eclipsed Domitila's third argument. She could picture him lying on his small bed positioned along the wall, there on the left... Not even a hospital bed, which would have made it so much easier to handle him. Instead, "the Master" stubbornly retained his tiny mattress on a plain wooden frame, like a monk. As was to be expected, the room was difficult to clean and the stench of infirmity had stuck to floor and walls for weeks after he was gone, despite Domitila's having piled every piece of furniture outside in the backyard for burning, right after the funeral. So, being left with this deadfully impractical vacated space—ahem, *dreadfully* impractical as a bedroom, located as it were on the ground floor—Afonso and she had done their best to find it a purpose which would enhance the glorious past of Arval while preserving the memory of the patriarch. That's how they had come up with the Equestrian Room idea. Every visitor to the mansion could now admire the most famous runner of Stud Arval without having to walk all the way to the stables' display area where it used to stand—or to rot, rather. And if the relics of *Introibo* now majestically stood in the very corner of the room formerly occupied by the master's cot, who could object? Was it not his favourite horse? And were the Arvals, or were they not, "horse people"!

"There you are Greta! Where have you been, Miss, may I ask? I was worried. No, this is no time for you to lie down by this horse again. Silly people will talk, don't you know? Come this way, to the kitchen. I say, Greta! Mummy has poured fresh

water for you, naughty girl. For the last time: not here! Oh,
you're so heavy, but I *could* drag you if I wanted. Don't make
me regret to have kept you in, or you'll be sent out, never to
be admitted again among us humans! There. That's better."

* * *

Several of the Arval siblings and children were sitting around
the vast rosewood dining-room table. It was a tradition. Not
only solemn family meals but also business meetings of the
family office team took place around that immense piece of furniture. Its many extra leaves were permanently set in, nobody
knew why, when a fifth of the length would have sufficed
for ordinary use. Visitors found it impressive, for sure. Mats
were spread to protect the mirror-like high gloss against pen
scratches and water stains. They were a dozen uncles, aunts,
nephews and nieces in charge of the studs, of the coffee and
sugarcane plantations, of the mansion (with its Romantic wing
decorated by Manuel de Araújo Porto-Alegre), of the São Paulo
flats (providing an income for the country seat of the family)
and of charitable works such as the shelter for addicts.

Since Afonso's incapacitation a year earlier, Domitila had sat
in the middle, opposite Henrique. He looked pleasantly tired.
As manager of Stud Arval, Domitila's youngest brother-in-law
had worked very hard to bring the family equestrian tradition
back to its former excellence. During the last years of Dom
Manuel's regime, standards had slowly lowered. In his late fifties, Henrique was a meek and congenial person. He'd always
been fond of horses but he also had a great way with people.
There was something inviting or comforting about him. Such a
rare quality: one felt totally unthreatened by him. It was good
to have him on her side. Some tried to appeal to Henrique's
kindness, even to manipulate him. But she wasn't blind.

"*Oitenta e três litros de café por pessoa !* Eighty-three. That's
how many litres of coffee every Brazilian drank last year."

Gastão, the second Arval son, was pushing again his rebranding strategy for Café Arval. He sounded as if trying to appear younger than he was—in vain. Perhaps, the rebranding was more about his own image.

"With merely 62 hectares, we're just too small to compete with large retail brands. Our only chance, we are told, is to turn our diminutive size into an asset, stressing that small means precious and beautiful."

"And how do you propose to achieve that goal, Gastão? Bury a pearl in every pack of Café Arval?"

As if not having heard Beatriz's comment, Gastão nodded at his son Gilberto who walked around the table, slowly distributing printed sheets of paper.

"Our advertiser told Father and me, 'Go vintage.'"

Born in 1970, Gilberto was barely ten years younger than his junior uncle Henrique, and again about ten years older than his cousin Rafael. His father Gastão was the second-born son, but he, Gilberto, was the eldest of the younger generation. He had officially taken over Café Arval from Gastão who gladly supported his son's initiatives.

"The advertising strategy includes reviving the old Café Arval iconic logo (displayed on your first page)."

Gastão couldn't help interrupting his son: "Ah, our old logo! I recall when it was dropped in the mid-sixties. Actually, it must have been in 1965, as I was twenty-three: I remember it because that same year, Elis Regina started presenting *Fino da Bossa*. Elis, the greatest Brazilian singer... I kept her signed picture in my room. Never mind—Afonso and I found the change exciting. We couldn't believe how easy it had been to convince Dom Manuel. Not only did he never object to the disappearance of horse and knight from the logo, but he even failed to detect that the stylised coffee leaves looked more like marijuana! What a psychedelic logo it was! Muahaha! But as Gilberto just said, take a look at the *old* logo designed before

World War One: a medieval knight leaning from horseback towards a black lady presenting him with a Café Arval china cup. It was clever at the time, but in the Sixties, it felt totally dusty, even reactionary. It had to go."

"And, is reactionary bad, Gastão?" Beatriz inquired. "Did our family not rightly 'react' against the jungle, against tribal violence, against paganism? I'm not ashamed of our history. Yes, we were once Portuguese colonists. And yes, we used slaves in our coffee plantation. But we treated them charitably. For years when serving Mass, you Gastão knelt under the *ex votos* in the mausoleum, some dating from the eighteenth century, put on the wall in thanksgiving for the recovery of the slaves who'd been sick or for their happy childbirth. So, why was the change of logo a good thing?"

Domitila smiled, guessing that the coffee strategy wasn't what bothered her sister-in-law. A deeper motive, she knew, fuelled resentment between poor Beatriz and Gastão. To foster schemes of his own, Gastão had committed in the eyes of Beatriz the "crime of lèse-majesté" — or "lèse-motherhood" rather — when supporting Afonso and Domitila's lay leadership at Dom Manuel's funeral against "Father" Luiz's involvement. Contrary to Beatriz's expectations, her priestly offspring had not run the show. Gastão had proved a worthy ally, so far. But Domitila had guessed his ambition to supplant her comatose husband as the senior Arval male in charge. This morning, along with his son Gilberto, he was displaying initiative and commitment to the family interests while her Rafael, *the* Arval heir, was absent yet again from this important family council meeting! Worse even, what if Gastão ever discovered Rafael's unhealthy relationship, and the prospect of his never begetting children to pass the estate on to? No, she would not get involved this time in the skirmish between Beatriz and her brother-in-law. She had other battles to fight for the good of the Arval clan of which *she* was at that time, like it or not, the senior representative.

Undeterred by his son's petition to focus again on the advertising strategy, Gastão pretended to answer his younger sister's question:

"Since you're asking me about *ex votos* for the slaves, dear Beatriz, sociologists could reply that our ancestors gave thanks to God because their cheap manpower was spared and oppression was secured. Come on Baba; is it not better for everyone to use tractors instead of slaves, while people of all ethnic backgrounds go about freely?"

Beatriz was not to be beaten. She smiled ironically at her daughter, announcing: "Did you just hear this good news, Maria? Since your uncle rightly cares for the welfare of innocent people of African descent, he will no doubt answer your invitation to join us at the prayer vigil next Friday outside the abortion clinic, where four out of five victims are people of colour."

"Dear me, I'm speaking tractors and she answers babies."

"Dad, no more tractors either, that's our point if you remember. May I please carry on?" Gilberto asked again. "On the second sheet, you'll find my proposed version of the revamped old logo. The advertising company designed it, of course. See, the knight is down from his horse, which he leads along the furrow made by a plough. The knight is now the one, with his other hand, pouring Café Arval in a mug held by an athletic samba dancer while walking. The revamped version brings together the revived Arval Stud and our original coffee trade. It sets our small coffee brand in a unique niche of politically correct excellence. We appear as the top environment-friendly and chic plantation, using thoroughbreds to draw ploughs and carts of coffee bags."

Samba? Domitila shivered at the thought that Gastão's new coffee logo might well be a veiled threat meant for her. Yes, he was implicitly pointing at her son's "partner." Why a samba dancer otherwise? But how could he ever know of "*Guiomar*"?

Beatriz protested: "What Gilberto, you don't mean to have two-hundred-thousand-dollar stallions draw ploughs, do you?"

"No Aunt Beatriz, not as long as they can win a race."

"But after," Gastão interjected, "better pull a cart than go straight to the slaughterhouse, don't you think? If you were a horse, Baba, I'm sure you..."

Beatriz interrupted her brother, as if not finding his humour to her taste:

"Henrique, tell them the suggestion is grotesque, please. After all, *you* are the Stud manager."

The youngest of the clan was not a man of confrontation. He smiled at his older brother's plan:

"That would be a decision to make together. Well, I'd be happy to keep our horses longer with us. They're our friends after all. And, if Gastão and Gilberto think it could improve the image of Café Arval. Just one thing though; I remember reading that some horses died after eating coffee husks. It can be toxic to them, so the article said."

"Fine, we'll make sure they don't eat any. Many humans die from drinking too much coffee anyway, don't they?" Gastão added, then realising that it wasn't the best selling argument for Café Arval.

Domitila thought it time to assert herself and concluded:

"This is food for thought, it seems to me. Can we all take a few days to ponder Gilberto's proposal—I see it detailed on the third page of his document—and decide next week? All agreed? Well, thank you. No other business before lunch, I assume?"

"Oh yes Tila, I nearly forgot to ask you. Is the mausoleum used for Mass again? I thought the quick low Mass at Dom Manuel's funeral last year was to be the last one for the foreseeable future, as Afonso notified us at the time. Being the one tasked with organising the paid visits to the mansion and its ancillary buildings, I would be glad to know if the rules have changed."

Domitila managed to hide a sudden tension in her limbs and on her face. She could sense that her sister-in-law's inquiry was not in the least impromptu.

"Yes, you're right Beatriz. Since Afonso and I became the sole occupants at the mansion, we sought more privacy than under Dom Manuel's regime. Naturally, as long as he lived, all of you went about as you pleased. It was great fun, I admit, to see siblings, nephews and nieces pop in at any time in the gardens, at the swimming pool and even inside the house. But especially with Afonso's condition, I thank you all for having respected our private perimeter over the past year or so. That still includes the chapel. Its tabernacle remains empty and no Eucharistic services take place, as Baba rightly remembers. Only booked visits are allowed from noon to 5pm."

"Oh, really? Why then was a *shepherd* in the chapel last Monday morning, if the Lamb of God is not offered or kept in there anymore?"

Some of the men around the huge table looked upset (Gastão and Gilberto), or apprehensive (Henrique), for all guessed that another battle had just started between the two sisters-in-law. The males felt like a hapless crew on a fishing boat suddenly becoming aware of missiles high over their heads crossing the sky in opposite directions, mutually fired by two distant warships at either side of the horizon. They knew from experience that it was too late to stop the ladies.

"Baba, if you mean *Shepherd* João, well, he came as my guest to offer some prayers. I hope that doesn't shock anyone."

Various male voices around the table assured, conciliatorily, that they were not shocked at all — especially, they thought, if assenting advanced their chances of moving on to lunch without further delay.

"So it was true?" Beatriz continued. "An Evangelical pastor gets invited to pray in our family mausoleum, while your own nephew, the only priest in the family, is denied his right to offer

Mass there? I didn't know that Protestants believed in praying
for the deceased, by the way. At least I've learnt something
today. Does Mr Hirt not have enough of Maristela church, or
will you invite his Novárvore Community to take over the Arval
Estate as happened with Leão Abbey?"

A couple of nephews and nieces looked embarrassed, some
uncles and aunts weary, while Henrique became passionately
engrossed in the examination of the revamped Café Arval logo
on his copy of the advertising document. Gastão and Gilberto
courageously rose from table, offering to let the ladies continue their private conversation with a reduced audience, now
that the official business of the day was completed. But Beatriz
wouldn't allow it. She went on:

"One moment Gastão, if you please. The Arval mausoleum is
family business no less than Café Arval, I reckon. I know that
it soon will be lunch time and the housekeeper must set the
table, but since we find ourselves discussing this topic, may I
ask why it has taken a year for Dom Manuel's funeral instructions to be shared, even though after his death? Only yesterday
did I discover an electronic copy of it in my junk folder, sent in
May last year by Henrique. I came across it purely by chance
and some of my nephews may have no knowledge of the letter.
Fortunately I have it with me today, on my phone."

Unease spread among the younger and older generations still
sat around the wide rosewood table. Some faces betrayed a hint
of annoyance, while others displayed curiosity. Domitila stared
at Henrique resentfully across the table. But he was transfixed
in the contemplation of the new Arval logo, unless it was the
old one — or whatever on the printed document required his
fullest attention. Gastão was still standing by the door of the
vast dining room. He walked back towards the table and spoke
with a concerned and pacificatory smile:

"Dear Baba, we're sorry that Father's funeral still is a sore
memory for you and your immediate family. The Sunday he

died if you recall, that evening Afonso and I searched Dom Manuel's desk and files in vain for his last instructions. It still is a mystery to me that his note was eventually discovered one month after his burial. Henrique and I found it, and I thought you had all received a copy of it long ago, as agreed with Afonso. Meanwhile, the morning after Father's death, on Monday 18th March precisely, all eleven of us, the Arval siblings, were around this very table for a family council meeting when the decision had to be agreed about funeral arrangements. As was announced to the congregation during the ceremony two days later, we wished your dear Luiz could have attended, but we understood that leaving Angola was very impractical, even dangerous given the volatile political situation at the time."

One of the younger faces looked puzzled: Hilda's, the daughter of Beatriz's youngest sister. Hilda was a glamorous twenty-seven-year-old, in charge, with her cousin Rafael, of the addicts' shelter: "Aunt Baba, sorry, but this sounds like Chinese to me. What letter are you talking about?"

"This is just my point. Why did no one tell Hilda and the younger generation? I'm not even sure that all of us siblings have received a copy. And yet, Father meant it for 'All.' Well, let me read it for you now from the picture on my phone. It's the original handwritten note, and very short as you will find. Dom Manuel wrote it on a legal form: '*Date: 14 April 2017; Purpose: Last will for my burial; Attention of: All. I ask Luiz kindly to organise my funeral, following as closely as possible the order of service at Uncle Honório's funeral. No flowers. Prayers. Thank you. Signed: Dom Manuel Arval.*'"

There was silence. Hearing the late patriarch's plain wishes quoted in the first person as if he stood in the room before them pricked the conscience of his progeny in various ways. Blushing, Hilda whispered into the ear of her cousin Maria, one of Beatriz's daughters, who nodded with a stern face and seemingly wet eyes. Gastão smiled with gravity: "Yes, again, one wishes Luiz

could have done the funeral. But what is past is past. Father
would want us to move forward, all the Arvals united. It's nearly
1pm I realise, and perhaps it's now time for setting the table, or
for departing and going about our respective businesses."

But Hilda stood up and with a shaking voice — was it sorrow
or indignation? — insisted: "Uncle Gastão, with respect, since
we the younger generation are now involved in the running of
the family estate, as I am with the addicts' shelter, we should
also be told the truth regarding such an important event as
Dom Manuel's funeral. Forgive my surprise. We all knew how
close our grandfather was to Luiz. Sometimes it hurt a bit; true.
Like, at the celebration for our first completed year running the
shelter, when Rafael and I had just given a speech about our
service among the addicts, Granddad, forgetting the occasion,
gave a toast instead 'to the joy of having Luiz back home on
holiday from seminary'! It was around this very table."

"That's just the way he was", Gilberto commented noncommittally.

"So, I won't deny that blunders occurred," Hilda went on.
"Perhaps that's also why we loved him. But I always assumed
that our grandfather would have wished Luiz to do his funeral.
It was never discussed, to my knowledge, because it seemed
the obvious expectation for one with so deep a Catholic faith,
and with only one priest among his many descendants. Now,
I'm not really familiar with the Latin Mass. In fact, Granddad
himself attended that old Mass only when Luiz visited; and by
the way, even Aunt Beatriz and Uncle José attend the *normal*
Mass in Portuguese. But surely we would all have wished Luiz
to preside at the funeral service, especially since it had worked
well in Latin at Uncle Honorio's funeral apparently. Since Luiz
had immediately bought his ticket to fly here for the funeral,
as Maria just told me, why was Dom Manuel's letter necessary
for the same order of service to have been used for him? And
finally, why did Uncle Afonso announce on the microphone,

during the funeral service, that 'we were all in union with Fr Luiz who was detained in Africa by his ministry but so much wished he could have attended?' There's a word for this, it seems to me; and it's not 'transparency.'" Hilda sat down, shaking.

After another embarrassing silence had spread around the rosewood table, Beatriz intervened: "Thank you for asking straightforward questions, Hilda. There's no secret — or there shouldn't be. None of my brothers and sisters was unaware of what you said. My own question is: Why was Padre Roque asked to do the funeral even *before* Luiz was informed of his grandfather's death? As Maria just told you, Hilda, daily flights from Angola were available to take him here on time and pre-side at the ceremony. It takes just eight hours, direct. Had his parish been on the *moon*, your cousin would have come to bury his beloved grandfather all the same! Furthermore, had there been *another* priest among the ninety-nine descendants, and had Dom Manuel asked him to conduct the ceremony in Portuguese if thought preferable for peace in the family, Luiz would have attended. He told me so. Instead, I was here in the vestibule when Luiz rang from Africa to speak with Uncle Afonso, the very afternoon of Dom Manuel's death. I heard Uncle Afonso answer him that 'Padre Roque was already booked for the ceremony.' It wasn't difficult to guess that your cousin had asked about the rite of the Mass when I heard your Uncle reply: 'Yes, in Portuguese. Because . . . That's what I'm used to.' And that was the end of it."

Unable to bear it any longer, Domitila broke her silence: "Here we go again. Beatriz, since you've chosen to drag even your nephews and nieces into this, showing little concern for peace within the Arval family, perhaps because you've been a Leão for too long, I must add for their information what you just failed to mention, namely, that Afonso and I had invited your son to proclaim the gospel and deliver the homily. Why do you suggest that we excluded him? This is unfair and offensive."

"Proclaim the gospel! What generosity! That's better than merely carrying the cruets for one Padre Roque, who'd first met our family less than a year earlier when he started his retirement a dozen kilometres away from Arval. 'Proclaim the gospel!' For God's sake Domitila, how could there have been the slightest hesitation about Luiz conducting the service himself from A to Z, with the younger nephews as altar servers, with as many of us as needed to sing the *Kyrie* and even, as Luiz had offered your husband, even translations of the epistle and gospel read in Portuguese by Afonso as the eldest Arval son! Your nephew Luiz is a *priest* Domitila, a *priest*; and despite being a Leão, and until Rafael changes his mind and applies for seminary—and we all pray for more to be called—Luiz is the *only* priest in the family. Was that not enough for him to be allowed to offer the Requiem Mass of his grandfather? Even without Dom Manuel's letter, which of us siblings was unaware that it was Dad's last wish? Why did you prevent it? Very well, I will tell you before everybody: the plain reason is that *you* wanted to be in charge, never mind the intention of the deceased."

Domitila allowed a few seconds of silence to elapse. Spectacularly composed, she merely cleared her throat before standing up. "Beatriz, you're going too far. Sorry all of you, but we must settle this now and some background is needed for the sake of accuracy. Three years have already passed since Afonso and I were requested by Bishop Joaquim to coordinate the training of the lay ministers of funerals. Soon we just won't have enough priests around here and it is the Bishop's wisdom to plan ahead and ensure that all will be given a Christian funeral when clergy become scarce. That means 'adapting the mentalities.' That's why he insisted that even when a priest is available there should be no Mass at funerals but only a service of prayer and reading led by lay ministers. If we don't start now, people will never be ready. Should the Arvals ask for an exception to the rule, when even Senator Fernandes Braga, a former Cabinet Minister, had no Mass for his funeral last year while his second cousin, a Jesuit priest, sat in the stalls?"

Domitila paused for a few seconds, looking around her with concern, as if unsure whether any of her relatives around the vast rosewood table could possibly be tainted with disloyalty toward the bishop. She finally stated the right attitude:

"Surely not. We support our bishops. Bishop Joaquim did us great honour when sitting in choir at the funeral and preaching before a five-hundred-strong congregation at the parish church—including the Minister of Sports and some non Catholic dignitaries, may I remind you—while Afonso and I conducted the service as per his instructions. Several people told us, in fact, how fitting and moving it had felt to have the eldest son officiate at his own father's funeral. Furthermore, Bishop Joaquim is full of compassion and pastoral sensitivity. As a long-time friend of our family (you may know that he was at seminary with my brother), Bishop Joaquim knew well the delicate situation with Luiz's traditionalist choice."

"I see nothing 'delicate' in my brother saying the *Pater Noster* in Latin. Even children understand it," Maria whispered into Hilda's ear.

"As I was saying, Bishop Joaquim was the one who suggested having Padre Roque, our nearby priest, say a simple Mass of Thanksgiving for Dom Manuel's long life, at the family mausoleum right after the official funeral service in the large parish church. And Luiz would have read the gospel and spoken—both times in Portuguese, not in Latin!—had he wished to come. As you remember, only the immediate family attended the burial and Mass at the mausoleum, while our guests and relatives made their way with Bishop Joaquim from the village church to the mansion where refreshments were offered. We joined them soon after to fulfil our important social duties. This is how we best handled the complex logistics of that day. We are sorry that Luiz could not attend, but as everybody can see, your dear son, Baba, would have been warmly welcome."

"And as only *you* fail to see, Domitila, if *your* darling Rafael were the priest of the family rather than my Luiz, your son would have done his grandfather's funeral, with Mass and burial."

*   *   *

How many young novices had stood by that thick eucalyptus door, Domitila imagined, waiting in awe for their abbot's appearance and decisions? She was not a Cistercian monk and yet, sitting outside Shepherd João's study, formerly the Chapter Room of Maristela Abbey, she felt a bit apprehensive. Why had her Shepherd referred to her description of facts as "her interpretation"? She saw nothing requiring "interpretation" in her sister-in-law's offensive behaviour towards her three days earlier. All she needed was her spiritual advisor's approval of her intended line of conduct. Thinking of it in her usual cell at the abbey the past evening, she had wondered with dismay whether Shepherd João hadn't become a little permissive over the past months. Yes, the Novárvore Community was committed to ecumenical dialogue. But he, as a leader, was growing a bit too tolerant of certain extreme Christian beliefs and practices. Of course she wouldn't object to Luiz saying one of his traditionalist Masses in the chapel of the former abbey. Why did he even ask? Better here than at the Arval mausoleum, still off-limits. But Shepherd João, she'd discovered, had been on email with Luiz for weeks, if not longer. They corresponded. That was perplexing. Hadn't he even invited her priest nephew to visit the Community and say a Mass, "for the sake of knowing better each other's traditions"?

"Sister!"

Domitila jumped. Unlike her fashionable Suede slingbacks, Shepherd João's plain sandals couldn't be heard against the tree-patterned *azulejos* on the corridor floor. Carrying his grandchild asleep in his arms—again—a gentle smile visiting his bearded face, the Shepherd pushed the eucalyptus door with one elbow, letting her in. He laid baby Oscar in his cradle, whispering some apologies for having kept Domitila waiting:

"I'm babysitting again for Agnieszka but she got caught in traffic. I waited for her on the driveway as she hadn't time to get out of the car. Still, you won't guess her warning as she drove off: 'Dziadziu, beware of that little popish boy; he'll turn you into a Catholic.' She likes to tease me because she comes from Wadowice, where John Paul II was born. Luckily the baby didn't wake up."

Drawing the curtain of the nearby window for deeper shade by his grandson's cot, the Shepherd sounded meditative, before surprisingly adding: "If a 'papist', a cute one he is... Barely three months old. Perhaps he'll become pope and will do my funeral. Oscar the First! But he'll want to reconcile me with the Roman Church before that. Well, well; the Spirit blows in mysterious ways."

Domitila wasn't sure if she'd correctly heard the last sentence whispered by the grandfather, or 'Dziadziu,' while he still stood at some distance from her. Had he just been provoking her? They both sat on wooden stools in the prayer corner of the vast room. After invoking the Holy Ghost, Shepherd João closed his eyes and they prayed in silence for a few minutes until with his warm voice, speaking low because of the sleeping baby, he announced:

"Sister Domitila, you'll be pleased to know that your nephew holds no grudge against you and your husband regarding Dom Manuel's funeral. Although he thinks a fault was committed, he finds that Dom Manuel should have expressed his funeral preferences to his entire family himself, rather than merely write it on paper. It would have spared all your family a lot of trouble, Fr Luiz confided. As I mentioned yesterday, he made contact with me a while ago. He means to spend a few days

here on his next visit home from Africa. After all, his surname
is the same as Leão Abbey."

Domitila kept silent. She was looking at the stylised wooden
dove in front of them, hovering above the thick carpet. Then
she thought she'd heard baby Oscar whimper.

"I was intrigued by this so-called 'traditional form of the
Roman Eucharist'," Shepherd João commented. "It's quite different from the Catholic services I have attended in the past.
Fr Luiz sent me the video of the funeral service he conducted
last year at his mission chapel over there in Angola, on the day
of Dom Manuel's funeral. Perhaps you've watched it already.
Your son Rafael liked it apparently. To me it felt strange, as if
bridging not only the Atlantic Ocean, but also several centuries
of Church history. I had never heard Gregorian chant, let alone
sung by an African choir. *Dies Iræ*, it was called. Quite exotic,
if not 'enchanting.' Further into the service, the intensity of the
silence was even more impressive as Fr Luiz lifted the wafer,
while his altar boy was holding the back of his black and silver
vestment. He said he'd scheduled it to coincide with the time
of burial in your family mausoleum, four hours later according
to the time zone. I think I've guessed, by now, what matters
most to your neph..."

Crying interrupted Shepherd João who rose immediately and
walked to the opposite corner of the room: "There, there, little
one. Are you rested now? Mummy will be back soon enough
and she's prepared this for you."

Domitila was surprised by the grandfather's dexterity as he
nestled baby Oscar in his left arm and, having uncapped the
nursing bottle with his right hand, started feeding the little
creature. Out of the blue, a very, very remote picture flashed in
her memory. Yes, she'd totally forgotten this. Luiz would have
been a few months old, barely, when Beatriz left him with her
for a week as she was going on holiday with José. Domitila
remembered how she'd nursed the two cousins, Rafael and Luiz.

And now, thirty-eight years later... Unsure whether the reminiscence made her happy or weary, Domitila felt that further spiritual guidance was better postponed as the baby feeding was, to her at least, a distraction. She thanked Shepherd João and, on opening the door, heard his gentle voice:

"Oh, dear Sister, I nearly forgot to tell you that Fr Luiz had been glad to use your silver sprinkler, he told me, for his funeral service last year. I watched him spread sacred water, after the Eucharistic liturgy, upon the black rectangular cloth representing his granddad's absent coffin. You'd given the utensil to him as an ordination present, he fondly recalled. Very thoughtful of you — a woman's touch indeed — to have had the brush made of hair from his grandfather's favourite horse."

IX

Swine Flu by Loch Ness

(2009, SCOTLAND)

OBJECT: PRELIMINARY DIOCESAN ENQUIRY FOR INTRODUCING
THE CAUSE OF BEATIFICATION OF BISHOP LENNOX WALLACE, LATE
BISHOP OF KINLOCHLOUR (2007–2020), SCOTTISH HIGHLANDS
ATT: THE RT REV FERGUS DOOGAN, BISHOP OF KINLOCHLOUR

ON THURSDAY 24TH MARCH 2023

Dear Bishop Fergus,

Thank you for reminding me that the third anniversary of Bishop Lennox's exemplary death will occur in five days. I will certainly attend the Memorial Service at the Cathedral. How could I forget that, knowing the high risk for people over seventy-five in particular and while being in good health, he exposed his life for your sake at the peak of the Covid-19 pandemic, when the Intensive Care Unit had given up on you, and he persuaded them to let him in and give you the Last Rites? They didn't dare deny him, the Bishop, access to his dying priest. Your recovery was nothing short of a miracle and the subsequent death of Bishop Lennox from Covid-19 and pneumonia made the headlines.

There is all the time we need to start the beatification process, as by canon law at least five full years must elapse between death and submission of the libellus. *Thank you for having asked me to gather the documentation.*

As per our conversation over the phone yesterday, please find enclosed the file you asked me about regarding the Rev Théophane Khang Dung, MSJS. As previously stated, it is an unnecessary addition to the Postulation Material, at least in my opinion. Your predecessor Bishop Lennox was a well-known ecclesiastical figure and the diocesan archives offer more than enough documentation to assess whether the presentation of the canonical libellus *should be attempted or not, (as laid out in* Sanctorum Mater, *the 2007 Vatican Instruction for conducting Diocesan inquiries in the Causes of Saints).*

As you will see, the brief diary of this rather ordinary priest from Vietnam, Fr Dung, adds no significant information of a doctrinal or moral nature. However, your personal connection with Bishop Lennox and Fr Dung can justify the inclusion of such data as an annex to the official list of sources. You will remember that the enclosed pages were sent to me by Miss Bridget McDiarmid, known to you as a worshipper in your former deanery of Glenangus.

I look forward to your comments and I hope to have the first draft sent to you before All Saints.

Kind regards, Ewan

Rt Rev Mgr Ewan Munro MA, BD, JCL,
Postulator, 31 Dalmarnock Rd, St Columba's
Presbytery, Kinlochlour — e.munro@rcdok.scot

P. S. You asked me what chances Bishop Lennox's cause had in Rome. Frankly, I've no idea. But if the first bishop "martyr of COVID-19" happened to be your predecessor, I'd be glad to have contributed to the beatification process (although it would feel strange to kneel before a picture of old Len surrounded by a halo, and to invoke his intercession).

MONDAY 2ND FEBRUARY 2009, INVEROVEN

His Lordship, my cardiologist and I have all given up on me. For once we seem to agree, although I gave up first. It took Bishop Wallace a bit longer. I had the advantage of having had to put up with myself for seven decades already, whereas he'd known me for less than two years, and only from a distance. His letter is to the point. He can't see why I wouldn't give the Host on the hand outside the Vietnamese Mass. This comes in

addition to my "earlier whims," he regrets, such as making the
Eucharistic ministers redundant and turning my back on the
people during the Eucharist. He calls me "stubborn and unpas-
toral" and finds that things must change. He's right, I'm hopeless.
But I just can't do it anymore. Over the past year my heart ached,
physically. My doctor confirmed it. His medical report reached
me last week with the Bishop's letter, coincidentally. Unless I
reduce significantly my workload and avoid stressful situations,
I'm warned, my heart will not take me very far.

I wish I could have pleased my superiors (and avoided stress,
to comply with the cardiologist's advice). I still don't know
exactly why I have generally disappointed them. I didn't do it
on purpose. It's just who I am. In Lourdes, Our Lady told St
Bernadette, "I am the Immaculate Conception"; and in Bethany
Our Lord told St Martha, "I am the Resurrection." I can't get
rid of the thought that, "I am the Disappointment." No, that is
pride again. I'm just ... disappointing. Today is my seventieth
birthday. As it happens, it's also the fifty-third anniversary of
my admission into the Missionaries of St Joseph of Saigon. I feel
the need to put in writing where I'm at. I think I will resume
my journal, interrupted at the end of my noviciate fifty-two
years ago. We were told at the time to keep a diary as a help in
monitoring discernment. I stopped the exercise after admission.
I wasn't good at it, unsurprisingly.

For about eighteen months now I have served as Chaplain to
the Vietnamese community in Glenangus, here in the Scottish
Highlands. Mgr Doogan is our Parish Priest, at St Margaret's,
in the town centre. He allows us to use one of his two auxiliary
chapels, St John Ogilvie's in the hamlet of Inveroven where
I live. I'm in a rented flat above the small Spar shop, a con-
venience store. Not at St John's Presbytery: that's where Vera
lives — Vera Kvidera. She arrived before me. Vera is Czech and
very motivated. In her early fifties, she's the Youth Officer for
the Glenangus deanery. She must take many initiatives because

there are very few youths around here, unless she counts as
one. She could be my daughter. Vera asked me once how I
catered for young people in Norway (my previous assignment).
My method was simple. I explained to married couples why
contraception is harmful (and abortion). It brought to the Vietnamese chaplaincy many youths who otherwise would never
have existed. Vera never asked me for advice again. I hope I
haven't disappointed her.

In the beginning, I resented Vera calling me "Dung." I
respectfully stressed that my name is pronounced "Dzung."
In Vietnamese it means "strong", "courageous." Dung is also a
woman's name in my language. Then it is pronounced "Dung,"
not "Dzung." It means "beautiful." But in English, I soon learnt
that "Dung" means "manure." People never quite got it here.
After a few months, I stopped correcting anyone. When reading
the announcements at the main parish Mass, concelebrated with
Mgr Doogan, Vera would always forget the right pronuncia-
tion of my name: "You can be reconciled by Dung at 5:00pm
on Saturday." Her routine Sunday morning joke kept the congregation cheerful. Later, Vera and I found a *status quo*. Mgr
Doogan spoke with her, and since then she refers to me as
"*Fr* Dung," rather than merely "Dung." I'm glad. Perhaps, "Fr
Manure" serves me well. The words of Our Lord comfort me
a little: dung is still useful, He once taught, when good salt is
spread upon it. Apparently they burn dung for cooking in the
Middle-East and salt makes dung combustible.

Now my flock. Of the six Vietnamese families whose needs
I was supposed to serve in Glenangus, one only still attends.
For how long? Second-generation refugees have either lost their
Catholic faith or prefer to attend Mass in English. It facilitates
their integration. Many more Vietnamese live in Glasgow, but
that's several hours away. The young adults don't want to spend
their lives in a rural area. I understand them. Several of them
gradually moved back to Edinburgh where their parents had

first arrived in 1980 and where there is more work. No wonder they leave Glenangus or even Kinlochlour—for all Vera's
efforts. With a town population of 3,400 souls, of whom 251
are Catholics officially, any good priest in Glenangus would
need to work very, very hard to fill his pews. I'm not a good
priest. I'm a disappointing priest.

Mgr Doogan is a good priest. He works hard. Perhaps,
because he's younger. That's also why he's the Vicar General of
the diocese. I used to work hard when I was young. My heart
was stronger then. I arrived in Norway in 1975 and lived there
until 2007. They granted me Norwegian citizenship. I wasn't
doing too badly in Kristiansand. We had nearly two thousand
people. The mass exodus from Vietnam made it a necessity to
find space and to support our refugees. Things settled down
in the 1990s. My religious superior expected a lot from us, but
it was good to be part of a team. I got sent to Bergen in 2001
as superior, on the West coast of Norway. I suppose I would
have lasted longer than six years in Bergen if it hadn't been
for that monstrance. Yes, that's when they started realising I
was hopeless. It was a beautiful item, silver and enamel. But I
just couldn't have a huge dragon circle around the Host as if
about to devour it. The dragon...

Ah, the lengthy discussions with the leading parishioners,
and with my fellow religious. Holy Scripture only mentions
dragons as evil. It's different with lions. The devil is a prowling
lion, but Christ is the Lion of Judah. He's not the Dragon of
Judah. Okay, there's *Nehushtan*, Moses' brazen serpent, but it's
not the same. They said in Vietnam dragons are symbols of
good and depicted as such on Catholic buildings and artefacts.
Had I forgotten it? Was I losing my Vietnamese identity? Had
I lived abroad for too long? Could I not see that my refugee folks needed every possible help, and that criticising this
well-known Asian symbol of the dragon was counter-pastoral?
I was wrong to ascribe to it a modernist tendency, since even

eighteenth-century Bishop Pigneau de Behaine was buried in
a Vietnamese dress with embroidered dragons, as witnessed
by the French Consul J. F. Parrot in 1983, when the French
cemeteries were destroyed by the Communists.

I was already in Norway, but I'd seen at close range the
"enormous red dragon" of the Book of Apocalypse, unleashed
on my country. To replace the dragon monstrance, I started
raising funds to have an affordable replica made of the famous
Loreto monstrance of Prague. It also has a dragon, spiralling
downward to the earth, with two clawed arms, two wings and
a long serpentine body; but vanquished by Mary and above
her, by the Eucharist. That's the kind of dragon I can tolerate
so close to Jesus in the Host. Mr Phan, the main benefactor
to our community, did not accept my opposition, though. The
dragon monstrance was a gift of his. The fundraising for my
Loreto monstrance dried up. With the little that had been raised
they bought a gilded Communion plate. A family brought it
to me in hospital as I woke up after my double-bypass heart
surgery. They thought it would cheer me up.

My provincial presented me with a promotion. He said our
community, the Missionaries of St Joseph of Saigon, needed to
expand in Western Europe. My experience as a senior member—I was sixty-eight—recommended me to implant our small
order in the United Kingdom. Vietnamese families were asking for our ministry in Scotland. Flying from Bergen to Aber-
deen takes just over an hour. Sadly he couldn't send anyone
to accompany me, but as soon as I would have established our
apostolate, more would join me. It's been eighteen months and
no one has come. No, I'm unfair; my superior allowed me a
dog. But the tenancy agreement for my flat forbids pets. Even
pet dragons.

The truth is, the dragon monstrance was not the only reason
for my transfer. They never said it, but I sense that young N. (let
me rename her "Bian" for discretion's sake) was my downfall.

What a sweet young lady. Can I write this down? Teenage pregnancy was taboo among us refugees. Bian conceived. I didn't blame her. I knew so well how tough it was for all of us "boat people," stranded on the Norwegian shore. Especially the young. What future? What consolations? Her procedure was already booked. I prayed and managed to persuade her to cancel the surgery and meet me instead at the Mission, to look at the options for her and the child. I meant to enquire about the father later on. On the date agreed, she was late and I rang her mobile: apparently switched off. That evening she texted that she hadn't been allowed to leave school to see me. Later on she avoided me, and no child of hers was ever seen. But she must have told her parents my advice to her. I think they resented me for having endangered the honour of their family which was saved, I fear, at the cost of an innocent life.

On my little desk as I write, there's a bottle of *Highland Black* 8-Year-Old Scotch. I don't like whisky, but I like beer less and wine is expensive. Someone dropped it nicely wrapped on the first pew at St John's, with my name on it and an unexpected "Birthday Boy" card. I found it after our small candle-lit procession, when scraping the wax off the tiles down the main aisle (in fact, the only aisle in that shoebox of a chapel). I don't know how they found out that my birthday was today. I'm a rather private sort of "Dung." But I owe it to the good soul to drink of it. Let us celebrate. It's dark outside and the wind is howling.

SATURDAY 7TH FEBRUARY 2009, INVEROVEN

It's all white outside, but a bit patchy. The snow stayed much longer in Bergen.

There's some whisky left; a little.

Why have I done it again? It's like a pattern. I feel it come, or unfold and take control of my will. I know exactly where it's taking me. I know it's not going to help. And yet, I end up online. Navigating the same site for nearly an hour.

I should start by blocking the access to the attic. That's how it normally starts. It's cold up there anyway. I tighten my scarf and put on my anorak, and climb the ladder. Once upstairs, through the dormer window and between the hills in the far distance, I catch a small portion of water. Loch Ness. I was told that it communicates with the sea. It's very silly, but the thought electrifies me, because in Vietnam the coastline is 3,444 km long (Norway's is only 2,650 km if skipping the fjords). So, glancing at this bit of Loch Ness and its bank opposite makes me feel as if I saw home. Home. I look at it until it's dark, and even later, then I keep staring at the few lights on the shore opposite. Then, like a robot, I walk down back into the flat. I don't even take off my outdoor gear and press the Start button on my laptop and in no time, I'm on it and I watch. While doing it, I hear a faint voice protesting: "No use! Bad! Don't do it Théophane." But I can't help it.

Writing it down isn't easy. The very embarrassment is an incentive, on the other hand. It makes me realise — as if touching with my own eyes — the darkness of consent. Yes, Fr Dung: do dare and confess the sequence. All right. Here it goes. First, *Google Maps*. Then type "Vietnam." Then . . . Then zoom. Zoom. Again zoom. Press "Satellite." Amazing! I see the colours and shapes. Then press "Street View." Very few streets are highlighted in the country. But in Saigon, every stretch of land is. I wait for the three-dimensional view to upload. It is still blurred. It sharpens. There. There it is. With the mouse now, drag and drop the little yellow man onto any street. He lands. I land. There I am. Home. I then "walk" randomly, moving the mouse across the city. I almost smell flowers or street cooking. I seem to hear the horns of buses and the shouts of cyclo riders, although those are fewer than in my youth. Sometimes I recognise a site, like yesterday: "Cho Quan Catholic Church." I prayed facing the statue of Our Lady of Lourdes, high up in her outdoor grotto. I'll go back there on Wednesday; for her apparitions. Her feast.

I know. It's shameful. There's no escape. I'm where God put me. I'm in Glenangus. Not even: I'm in the hamlet of Inveroven. I'm above the Spar shop. I can hear the customers. The poodle of Mrs Heggins is barking. He doesn't like to be left outside in the cold wind. Neither do I. His mistress was surprised that a Catholic priest could fix the handrail by her front door. Speaking of old women, I found who gave me the whisky. It wasn't Vera. No, it's the very discreet lady who does the flowers at St John's. Miss McDiarmid. Bridget. She apologised profusely for the casual "Birthday Boy" inscription, saying all the respectable cards for seniors were gone from the shelf at the Spar shop. I never spoke with her much, despite her attending my Mass daily. Perhaps, because she's not Vietnamese. Thinking of it, why would I cater only for my fellow countrymen, if others ask me?

SUNDAY 15TH FEBRUARY 2009, INVEROVEN

I was given a book. It was printed in Saigon in 1921, five years after the first Vietnamese bible. It's a Roman altar missal. I'm looking at it, open on my desk by my laptop. How this volume arrived here, in the Scottish Highlands, is strange and simple. Miss McDiarmid took me yesterday to an event in Inverness, a small rally for Catholic families. The trip lasted over two hours one way because she drives slowly; and my heart condition makes me unfit for holding the wheel, lest I collapse. She had arranged to introduce me to acquaintances of hers, the Billards. They live half way between Glenangus and Perth. Mr Jacques Billard is a hotel manager in the Cairngorms National Park. He's French but his wife is Cambodian, although she was adopted by a French couple in 1975 and raised as a French girl. They home educate seven young children. You can tell their mum's Asian.

Some years ago, Antoinette (that's Madame Billard), made contact again with her relatives settled in France like her. Among various souvenirs she was given some items belonging to her

late great-uncle, a priest in what was then French Cochinchine,
now partly Cambodia. Hiding his priestly identity, Antoinette's
relative let himself be deported by the Communist Viet Minh to
the infamous "Camp 113" near Lang-Kieu, run most cruelly by
French political commissar Georges Boudarel, aka "Dai Dong",
a former Marist student. The priest ministered there in secret
until his death two years later. When hearing through Miss
McDiarmid where I was from, Antoinette prepared the altar
missal and gave it to me, nicely wrapped inside a case with the
label "Saigon Missal." I felt I couldn't accept, but she said it's in
Latin and too big for her to use. She added that her great-uncle
would be glad if a priest from the same part of the world could
use it. Of course I can't. I was ordained in 1965, when the rite
of Mass was changing every year until the new missal of Pope
Paul VI came in force in the 1970s. I've always used it since.
On second thought, I took the book in response to her kind
gesture and in memory of her courageous great-uncle.

It's snowed again this morning. Miss McDiarmid brought
a friend of hers to my 4pm Mass. In his twenties, he's called
Adam and works in computing. He also sings at Mass, he men-
tioned. We had tea together afterward, with the last remaining Vietnamese family. Every Sunday morning I must help at
Mgr Doogan's main parish Mass at St Margaret's, in Glenangus.
But here at St John's we were eleven in total this afternoon.
That's my record number since January. For the sake of the
non-Vietnamese, I translated the readings into English. Miss
McDiarmid said she liked the fact that I always say in Latin
the Creed, the Our Father and outside of Lent also the Gloria.
She and her friend made a point to kneel down when receiving
the Host (on the tongue like my parishioners do). As she left,
she gave me a thin book by an Eastern Catholic Archimandrite,
one "Anatolijus Teiloras" called *Digital Communion, a Modern
Invention*. I had a brief look at it and, contrary to what the title
suggests, it's nothing to do with the internet or with computer

evangelisation. It's about using one's fingers to take the Host and put it into one's own mouth. Archimandrite Anatolijus Teiloras says that it never happened anywhere in the Catholic Church until the late 1960s. It's a modern invention, he writes.

It's past 10pm and I've resisted going to the attic or using *Google Maps*. I've been reading this altar missal instead. On the first page inside, I see the words: "*Nihil Obstat, Victor-Charles Quinton, MEP, Vicaire Apostolique de Cochinchine Occidentale, Saigon.*" I remember many prayers from this rite. The responses at the beginning of Mass. The *Confiteor*. And sounds as well, like the bells at the *Domine Non Sum Dignus*, and gestures like lifting the chasuble of the priest at the elevation. A pity these things were lost.

It must be my imagination. I mean, I brought my nose close to the inside of the book and it smelt of jasmine. My left hand rests against the leather cover, my fingers spread wide across it. Is it not a piece of Vietnam I'm holding?

MONDAY 23 FEBRUARY 2009, INVEROVEN

I've now truly disappointed Vera. I'm so sorry. I put a purple frontal on the altar. It struck me that its bare thick concrete legs were better covered. Coloured material helps remember the liturgical season, I feel. I also put six small candlesticks and a matching crucifix donated by Adam, the friend of Miss McDiarmid. The crucifix is free-standing, unlike the small flat one normally lying on the cloth next to the microphone. The new items are set upon two long painted wooden boxes Adam made. He calls them "gradines." Finding me in the sacristy, Vera asked me to take everything down before her youth meeting in the parish room, (despite Adam being even younger than her four young adults). I asked her why, as she was not having a prayer service this time, and since my additions improve the altar. She said she liked "noble simplicity" and should not wish her young people to get weird ideas when walking through the chapel. I dared to enquire why they would not access the room from her front door, since the meeting room is part of the presbytery where she lives. She looked flushed, saying she won't mix work and private life. Perhaps I should have left it at that.

Instead, I surprised myself when I replied that it wasn't very considerate of her to ask me to undo the arrangement; and that her young people could kindly do it if they wanted, provided they put things back in place, because with my heart condition I mustn't carry heavy items like the two "gradines." Vera looked at me with a rather awkward smile and said nothing for a while. I was mortified. On the vestment press she saw the box with the missal of Antoinette's great-uncle. Reading aloud the label "Saigon Missal," she asked if the "stuff" was all about my Vietnamese rite. Not sure what to answer, I agreed that it was the way I had been taught Mass at Saigon. Happily she changed the subject, asking if I'd ever visited Culzean, a beautiful castle on the coast, south of Glasgow. Of course I hadn't. I would enjoy it, she suggested, because of a rolling-uphill illusion on the road over there. At the "electric brae," cars in freewheel seem to move *up* when actually going *down*. I said that sounded truly interesting. Even though I don't drive and thus couldn't go on an excursion that far south, I'm grateful to Vera for having patched things up between us.

Last night in my attic, through the dormer window, I looked at the opposite bank of Loch Ness again. My imaginary Vietnam across the water. Should I go back there? Could I? After all, a sick old man is no great danger to the Communist regime. My heart aches.

Yesterday, Miss McDiarmid took me to the Billards. It's fifty minutes from Glenangus. I was very glad to get to know Jacques and Antoinette better. The children played the flute and the piano and even the violin. Antoinette had cooked lemongrass tamarind chicken, "a Vietnamese treat," she announced. Their home is consecrated to the Sacred Heart. It's many years since I've met a family like that. Before we left, all came to Confession to me. I was in the dining-room with the door open and they came one by one from the lobby and the sitting-room.

Henri, the eldest son, asked if he could serve my Mass. But Jacques his father explained: "Fr Théophane says the *Novus Ordo*, Henri. You wouldn't quite know the responses and gestures." Antoinette saw that I was perplexed. She gave a very gracious smile, commenting: "We drive to Sterling where there's a traditional Latin Mass every Sunday at 5pm. But one hour fifteen minutes to get there is very long for the children." Miss McDiarmid and I had got into the car and were about to drive off when Henri knocked at my window and asked: "Fr Théophane, could you please say the traditional Latin Mass, and I will serve it for you?" Yet again, someone I'm disappointing, I thought on the way back. A child, this time.

SUNDAY 1ST MARCH 2009, INVEROVEN

Adam sang the Kyrie and the Creed in Gregorian chant this afternoon. He told me not to worry about the gradines. He will take them down and up again whenever Vera needs the altar stripped. I'm relieved, because I can't afford a conflict with her. Especially after Mgr Doogan's phone call. He gently enquired how I was doing, apologizing that there's never much time to chat when I come and help at his main parish Mass in Glenangus. He was a bit annoyed that I had waited nearly a month to show him the letter sent by my cardiologist. He permitted me to remain at Inveroven on Sunday mornings if I felt too weak, and even suggested that instead of me Vera could help with Communion at his Saturday vigil Mass. I feel a bit guilty to let those two do all the work in Glenangus, while I'm left with only the Vietnamese 4pm Sunday Mass. I insisted that I could still come to hear Confessions, as that isn't so strenuous. But he preferred not anymore, for my sake, apart from the penitential service before Easter. Jacques Billard attended my Mass this afternoon with a young colleague from his hotel. I was happily surprised to see Jacques, assuming he only attended old Latin Masses. He sang with Adam — adding a third "*Eleison*" for each invocation, so that nine "*Kyrie*" were sung in total. I'd forgotten it used to be the way. We were fourteen, a record. Realising that the majority of us now were native or fluent English-speakers, I told my congregation that I would dispense with the Vietnamese readings from now on. I also said the Offertory in Latin, and the Eucharistic Prayer in a low voice, as it's less tiring for me. In truth I felt tired the whole day.

TUESDAY 10TH MARCH 2009, INVEROVEN

What I have done?

I'm afraid, and thrilled. If it hadn't been for his feast . . . I had double-checked his dates: St John Ogilvie, SJ (1579–10 March 1615). Our little St John's Chapel was built in 1976 in preparation for the canonisation of this Scottish martyred priest, and blessed the following year, just thirty-two years ago, on the anniversary of his martyrdom. Miss McDiarmid remembers the occasion proudly. It was the first church built in the newly established Diocese of Kinlochlour. Adam wasn't born of course, but he showed me the old video. He was the one, I think, a fortnight ago, who first aired the idea: "Would it not be a wonderful tribute if Holy Mass that day could be offered in the very rite St Ogilvie died for." I ventured that surely the martyr had died for Christ, the Church and the Mass, not for a liturgical rite in particular.

Back at the flat though, I don't know why, I felt uneasy and sad.

Well, it can't be undone now. I suppose it went all right, rubrics-wise. Of course I had been trained in that rite and had said it — or its slightly modernised version — for the first five years of my priestly life. When did the Last Gospel disappear? I can't remember. I had rehearsed for two weeks. Not at St John's, for fear Vera would see the maniple on my left wrist! No, but in the attic. I dusted the broken chest-of-drawers and dressed it as an altar. It's about the right height. Once, on a full moon evening, I didn't even need the electric light on, just the candles. Adam was serving and was deeply moved when he left: "Just like under Penal Times, Father." I wonder how many priests, like me, had never been told about this provision by the Holy Father. Two years ago apparently, permission was given to all priests in the Latin Church to say the traditional Latin Mass. Jacques gave me the document. *Summorum Pontificum*, it's called. Of course, I'd vaguely toyed with the idea before, but it was like daydreaming, as I would never have disobeyed the Church. When I saw it was allowed . . .

It's late. I left my desk and went up into the attic again, looking at the opposite bank of Loch Ness. So, there it was. I'd wondered how far the dragon had followed me, after Saigon, Kristiansand and Bergen. Now I know that dragons can fly, unless he swam from Norway and made its way into Loch Ness. A clever dragon. A cunning beast. That silvery band in the distance, attracting me as a symbol of my lost motherland and youth, *that* was the dragon. A holy angel unmasked it. I wouldn't have guessed. If anything, I had flirted with it. It had half hypnotized my soul. I think I remember now where *home* is. Why have I barked for so long in the silence of my heart, like the poodle of Mrs Heggins left outside the warm shop? Am I let in again, now? Have I disappointed the dragon?

"*Thou shalt walk upon the asp and the basilisk: and thou shalt trample under foot the lion and the dragon.*"

SUNDAY 15TH MARCH 2009, INVEROVEN

Not only the entire Billard family, but also two more, friends of theirs, attended the 4pm Mass this afternoon. The parents of the largest family — ten children! — said they had seen me at the Catholic rally in Sterling last month. Exactly four weeks ago then, when to me it feels like years have gone by since. They congratulated me on my first Old Rite Sunday Mass. I announced to the congregation that I would now use the "Saigon Missal" every Sunday. After Mass, the parents of the remaining local Vietnamese family were the only ones who asked for clarification. They didn't mind the change but wanted to make sure they understood what was happening. Antoinette gave them red booklets produced by *Sursum Corda*, the Scottish association promoting the old Latin Mass. It's surprisingly easy to use, with the English on one page and the Latin on the opposite page, including small pictures of the postures of the priest at the altar to check which part of the Mass one is at.

We were thirty-two in total, including nineteen children. Henri and two other boys served. Jacques, Adam and another man sang the Gregorian chant. I did a poor job with incensation. But the Offertory singing was... I don't know how to describe it. Antoinette, another mum and two daughters sang a motet, accompanied on the violin by a Billard daughter. Perhaps it was because the melody reminded me of my time in formation in Saigon. I can't recall having heard Mozart's *Panis Angelicus* since. They were a bit concerned when they saw me leave the altar and sit for a while. Adam was making signs for me to resume the liturgy, assuming, as he explained afterward, that I was waiting for the New Rite Offertory procession to assemble in the tiny church porch. I didn't tell anyone about the pain in my chest. More intense.

TUESDAY 24TH MARCH 2009, INVEROVEN

Mgr Doogan came to see me yesterday. I've been resting since his visit, but I feel better now. He turned up in the sacristy as I was polishing the old chalice Miss McDiarmuid found for me in an antique shop in Kinlochlour. I must have it and its paten "consecrated" by the Bishop before use, Adam insisted. Monsignor asked if I knew of an "Extraordinary Form Sung Mass" scheduled at 4pm at St John's last Sunday. Not being familiar with the expression he used, I genuinely said that it must have been a mistake, because only my usual Mass had taken place. His brand new phone can connect to the Internet and he showed me the announcement on the website of *Sursum*

Corda. There were also a couple of pictures from the Mass, showing only the back of my chasuble — thank God — but St John's Chapel was unmistakably recognisable. He smiled wryly, commenting: "The celebrant may not be you, of course. But if you see him, make sure he asks me before he says another Extraordinary Form Eucharist in this deanery." I felt guilty, as if I had tried to lie to him, and fell onto the chair I normally use for Confessions. I explained the misunderstanding caused by my use of the expression "Saigon Missal" so far, and pointed at the box with the book in it. Dragging it out on the vestment press, he opened it with great caution and turned the pages as if they were contaminated. He asked for how long I had been using that missal and I caught a hint of satisfaction on his face when hearing it had been my second Sunday Mass only. He was perplexed to learn that my numbers in the pews had nearly tripled, that the Offertory collection was tenfold, while the average age of the congregation had plummeted.

"From the pictures, it seems Vietnamese have multiplied overnight," he noticed, "although I see many non-Asians as well, including ... My word, this young fogey *is* our Adam Brown, unsurprisingly, the diocesan webmaster: there, near your little organ!" Brown, I think that's the surname Monsignor spoke. Certainly his tone of voice was complimentary, with perhaps some innuendo that I had on purpose attracted diocesan staff to my scheme. It embarrassed me because I'm far too hopeless to scheme anything, and because Adam's function in the diocese was news to me. "On the other hand," Mgr Doogan remarked as if talking to himself while walking across the nave of the chapel, "more money coming could get the Vietnamese Chaplaincy out of the red soon, and even match the running costs of St John's Presbytery." I must have looked very perplexed, not quite seeing how Vera would have me stay in her house. He explained: "Did I not mention it earlier? Vera might be needed in town where there are more youths around, and where she can help with the liturgy. You, Fr Dung, could move into her premises, having more space to accommodate your activities, if your little fad turns into a sustainable venture. But tell me, does your heart condition really allow this? I recall you were told to take it *very* easy, weren't you? Or else, will your confreres at the Saigon Missionaries of St Joseph send you an assistant, as originally planned?" I was standing outside by his shining purple Volvo car, unable to find an answer. As he started reversing (surely an electric engine, to be so silent), he added through the window that as to the "Saigon Missal," he would of course need to report to the Bishop, who is "the moderator of the liturgy in his diocese."

SUNDAY 29TH MARCH 2009, INVEROVEN

Thank God for Bishop Wallace. He wrote to me a kind letter allowing me to continue. I have thus offered this afternoon my third Sunday Mass in the traditional form. We were forty-six in total. I'm exhausted because I rose one hour earlier due to the beginning of British Summer Time this morning, and because yesterday we spent hours veiling the statues and crucifixes. It's "Passiontide." Why have I never done this before, I mean, since my early years in Norway? A miracle occurred earlier last week when Mrs Heggins, having heard of our project through her neighbour Miss McDiarmuid, offered to sew the purple material herself: "As a Presbyterian, I find it very natural to hide sacred statues and images," she said. Since her church in Inveroven got shut down last summer, she'd been helping Miss McDiar-muid with the flowers at St John's. But since flowers are not permitted on our altar in Lent, she has time on her hands, she assured. She says we're all Christians after all, and we still have "Quinquagesima" like she used to. She's good friend with Catholics, she insists. Her second-cousin, a Monsignor, is an official at the Congregation for Divine Worship in Rome and got her a priority ticket into the Vatican Museum, so that all her fellow-tourists were amazed.

Now His Lordship's letter, clearly a blessing from Our Lady on her feast.

"Wednesday 25th March, 2009, Bishop's House, Kinlochlour

"Dear Dzung,

"In my letter to you last 30th January, I stated my dissatisfaction with your liturgical innovations, e.g. no hand Communion, no Eucharistic ministers, celebration back to the people etc. Since then you have started using the Extraordinary Form missal. In this context, I do not object to your aforementioned liturgical preferences inasmuch as they fit with the older missal. I am pleased that you have shared with Mgr Doogan your projects for the Vietnamese Chaplaincy. While you have lost some of the families you came to minister to originally, I understand that more worshippers have come since. Time will tell how viable this is.

"You may know that over the past eighteen months I have been looking for the best location for a regular Extraordinary Form Eucharist, as asked by His Holiness Pope Benedict in his Motu Proprio *Summorum Pontificum*, in force since 14th September 2007. Fr Ewan Munro came back from Rome last autumn, having completed his Licentiate in Canon Law. He had started learning the Extraordinary Form at my request and was scheduled to offer it for the first time in public on 7th July at the Cathedral. But his workload at the Tribunal might not allow him to become proficient by then. Since you have taken an interest in this form of the Mass, I am transferring to you the mission originally envisaged for Fr Ewan Munro as Priest in Charge of the Diocesan EF Sunday Mass, effective this Sunday.

"For the sake of continuity, this Mass will continue in its present setting, namely, every Sunday at 4:00pm at St John's Chapel, Inveroven, which comfortably seats fifty. There is sufficient parking and it is just under one hour drive from Kinlochlour, allowing convenient access for anyone in the Diocese. Mgr Doogan will sort out the financial arrangements with you. After a three-month trial period, we will see whether a second

priest from your order should be asked to join you, which
might necessitate your moving into St John's Presbytery.

"It goes without saying that everything must take place in
full compliance with the Diocesan guidelines and customs, and
that you must turn down any pastoral requests which would
endanger your precarious health.

"With my blessing,

Lennox +"

26TH APRIL 2009, GOOD SHEPHERD SUNDAY, INVEROVEN

Can it be already a month since I last opened this journal?
Time literally flew. Although I still feel very tired, Holy Week
was a success. Nothing would have been possible without the
people's support. I was too weak and too forgetful of the old
ways to be much involved in the preparation of the ceremonies.
I did my best to sing, but that was particularly tiring and stressful. Thus, after Maundy Thursday, I had to do everything as Low
Masses rather than sung. Adam conducted several motets and
Will, the fourteen-year-old son of the Billards' friends, acted as
Master of Ceremonies. It brought back very, very old memories
from my formation years at the MSJS in Saigon.

Jacques and Antoinette insisted that I should spend six full
days of rest at their hotel in the Cairngorms National Park. I
stayed in a very comfortable suite and they had arranged for
me to offer Mass privately at their house. My altar server Henri
turned eight on my last day. A few days earlier, to his parents
probing what sort of birthday present he would like (he's fan
of Greek weaponry since watching *The Fall of Troy*), the boy
had answered: "Can I have a Saigon *missile*, like you once
said is hidden in Fr Théophane's church?" He didn't understand why all of us adults laughed, but as birthday present he
got a recurve bow, for now. Young Hélène will make her First
Holy Communion next month. I have very little to teach her.
She's been well catechised by her parents already. They lent

me fascinating books about what happened over the past sixty years in the Church. I feel a bit silly writing this. Was I on the moon during all that time? On the contrary, was I not fully active among my flock in Kristiansand and Bergen, and here? But, mysteriously, I wasn't really conscious of what had been going on behind the scenes. Did I block it out?

The parishioners are making plans for after the summer. Those with young children fear that retaining the 4pm time for Holy Mass will be very difficult for the younger ones to keep quiet and be recollected. Would not a 10:00am Mass be possible, they hope, since St John's is not used in the morning either? They also suggest I enquire now with my superiors about having an assistant sent in September. They have put together records and statistics of our congregation since the very first "Saigon Missal" Mass. The announcement on the diocesan website boosted our numbers before Easter. Attendance went down a bit since, but is now regularly over sixty, one third of them being children. I have received two requests for traditional baptisms in the forthcoming months. People have heard of its triple exorcism and seek it for their children. Five young adults are now regulars. Four come from Kinlochlour and one from Perth. They have started a newsletter which I only need to proof-read. They also want to found a *Juventutem* group.

I came back last week and do not feel the same urge to write regular accounts in my journal. Perhaps do I not need it as much as before. I end this entry here, since I must read further *Iota Unum*, a monumental book by Professor Romano Amerio, praised by *L'Osservatore Romano* two years ago. It's warm enough outside for me to sit in the garden. Elvis, Mrs Heggins' poodle, normally plays on the grass by my chair. I wave at his good mistress on her neighbouring lawn separated from the Spar shop garden by a very low fence. She knits a sort of a monkish hooded jacket for Elvis, unless it is for the youngest Billard baby boy. Elvis was naughty yesterday, unrolling the thread of light blue wool across the lawn until it caught in the *Mary Queen of Scots* rose bush. As a punishment Mrs Heggins made him skip his *Royal Canin Chicken Biscuit* afternoon snack. But good behaviour over the following ten minutes or so was rewarded with Elvis' pardon, mercifully. I wonder if Mrs Heggins wasn't the one suffering from the sentence more than Elvis.

SUNDAY 14TH JUNE 2009, INVEROVEN

The First Holy Communions of three children this afternoon was a beautiful occasion. Young Katherine Docherty, one of the candidates, was not part of our regulars. But her parents preferred that she should receive on the tongue, even though it meant being separated from her classmates from Glenangus. They might come again.

I'm worried by a circular email from our Parish Priest Mgr Doogan, the Vicar General. I insert it here.

"To all clergy in the Kinlochlour Diocese.

"Brethren, Bishop Lennox asked me to make sure you all have heard the alarming news from the Scottish Government today, quoted below.

"*Scotland has 35 new laboratory-confirmed cases of Influenza A (H1N1) today bringing the total number of cases in Scotland to 498. It can also be confirmed that one of the patients who had been in hospital and had been confirmed as suffering from the virus has died today. The patient had underlying health conditions. The new cases are in Greater Glasgow and Clyde (32), Highland (1), Forth Valley (1) and Grampian (1) NHS Boards. There are currently ten people with Influenza A (H1N1) being treated in hospital. Across Scotland there are 175 possible cases being investigated. The Scottish Government is not aware of any further school closures at present.*

"No doubt you have followed the news about the unstoppable spread of this new virus across the world since April.

After this first H1N1 casualty in Scotland today, our country must prepare to face responsibly the very serious threat of the so-called 'Swine Flu.' This includes us, Catholic clergy. Avoiding contamination is our primary duty to the people entrusted to our care. Please urge your parishioners who show any of the symptoms to stay at home. As a preventive measure, it is highly recommended to distribute Holy Communion on the hand rather than on the tongue, even though this latter option is used by only a minority.

"Please be on your guard and await updates from the Diocese.

"F. Doogan, V. G."

WEDNESDAY 1ST JULY 2009, INVEROVEN.
FEAST OF THE MOST PRECIOUS BLOOD.

I prayed that it might not come to this, but here we are. His Lordship emailed all clergy this morning. I surely don't want to disobey him. But over the past few years, it has become more and more painful for me to give the Host on the hand. I just can't see how I can account for the loss of the small fragments remaining in the palms of the communicants. The Church teaches that each one of them is God, as long as visible to the eye. My now stable congregation of sixty-two souls at St John's would not wish to receive on the hand anyway. My only hope is in the word "I recommend" chosen by His Lordship. This means "I advise", not "I command." There is a good case for an exception for the Traditional community here. And yet, how am I so bold? It doesn't sound like the Fr Dung who arrived here less than two years ago. Can I disappoint my good bishop?

"Diocese of Kinlochlour, 1st July 2009

"Catholic Church Regulations: Swine Flu Pandemic

"During the current Swine Flu epidemic, in keeping with the latest guidelines that I have received, I recommend that the following measures be implemented in Catholic Churches throughout the diocese from this weekend:

1) The Sign of Peace during Mass. Instead of a handshake, members of the congregation are asked to join their hands together, as in prayer, turn to their immediate neighbours, bowing slightly and saying 'Peace be with you.'

2) Holy Communion is to be given only on the hand, not on the tongue or from the chalice.

3) Ministers of the Sacred Host are asked to ensure their hands are washed with sanitizers (provided) before and after ministering communion.

"These regulations will remain in place until further notice. It is hoped that the reasons for this temporary policy will be understood and appreciated. They have been made out of particular pastoral concern for the vulnerable, namely, the elderly, children and those with underlying health problems.

"Bishop Lennox Wallace +"

MONDAY 6TH JULY 2009, INVEROVEN

Mgr Doogan heard that I had given Holy Communion on the tongue yesterday. He emailed me in the evening: "As Vicar General I must warn you that noncompliance with the Bishop's decision compromises the future of the *Missionaries of St Joseph of Saigon* in the Kinlochlour Diocese. It is essential that all our clergy should follow the same rules, for fear of harming the unity of the presbyterium."

What terrible words... He must know that the MSJS are present nowhere else in the entire country. If we lose Inveroven, we lose everything. And just when things were so promising. I slept very little last night. Having taken advice from my Provincial and from some parishioners, I have emailed the following to His Lordship this morning:

"Your Excellency,

"I need to submit to your judgment the difficulty in which I find myself in the current Swine Flu pandemic. I have received your circular emails to all clergy, including the latest one last week indicating your recommendations. As a Catholic priest I take obedience to the local Ordinary and to the local ecclesiastical authorities very much to heart. Some of the regulations recommended are not difficult for me to apply, but I am afraid the one about Holy Communion in the hand is. The reason is that the Extraordinary Form of the Mass does not envisage another mode of giving Holy Communion than on the tongue. I know that the faithful attending the EF Mass (not only here but in other countries as well) would rather make a spiritual Communion than not receive on the tongue.

"I have asked my Provincial in Norway how this difficulty had been solved in other dioceses where we serve under the same pandemic threat. He said that Bishops haven't made Communion in the hand a *sine qua non* condition.

"As diocesan Bishop, you are the one regulating Eucharistic worship all across the diocese, including for the EF worshipping communities. If you find that current circumstances make it too risky for them to receive on the tongue at all, I will indicate your decision to our good people at St John's. If one wished to make sure the diocese or the parish would be safe from public liability, the faithful here could be required to sign a form stating that they receive in the traditional way at their own risk.

"I understand that the pandemic threat might increase, reaching a stage when Holy Communion may be altogether suspended in both forms of the Roman rite, and also in the Ukrainian rite (every other Sunday in the Glenangus deanery, where the Body and Blood of the Lord are given with a spoon directly in the mouth of each communicant). Spiritual communion may then become the only option. Please let me know what you would want me to do in these delicate circumstances. I dread disappointing you.

"If I may mention, the risk of contamination depends on the number of persons in tactile contact with the Sacred Species, and also on the number of items touched by every such person. In the Extraordinary Form of the Mass this risk is greatly lessened because only the celebrant touches the Hosts and Sacred vessels in general, and since after Consecration he will not touch with his thumbs and forefingers any object or item other than the Host(s). Also, I'm used to not touching the communicant's tongue when I give him the Host. I have however been cleansing my fingers with the special anti-germs sanitizer provided at the parish last Sunday—this just before Mass and another time just before Consecration. I have been interrupting the Mass once more for cleansing my fingers during the distribution of Holy Communion.

"I am sorry for the length of this message, but I can't see how to do without presenting to you the practical elements in detail.

"Yours respectfully,

"Fr Théophane Dung, MSJS"

SATURDAY 29TH AUGUST 2009, CAIRNGORMS PARK LODGE.
BEHEADING OF ST JOHN THE BAPTIST.

Still breathing, nearly two months later. I have spent the past fortnight at the hotel with the Billard family. I just couldn't cope any longer. I did two baptisms, but a change of setting was becoming urgent, I was advised. The Billards wished to take me to the Edinburgh Festival but I simply couldn't face it. I would have liked it very much, though. Last summer I had accepted the invitation of a Vietnamese family to attend the Military Tattoo at the Edinburgh Castle. In the dark, I recall, a young private wearing a black uniform started playing the violin; alone. *The Gael*, that music was called. He felt so solitary in his tight circle of light, poor boy, and yet, his tune gave hope to all of us. Then an older and bulky sergeant joined him with a bagpipe and the circle of light broadened around them. One felt more confident as the music grew louder. Only after that were all the lights turned on at once, revealing dozens of soldiers in splendid parade uniforms (white straps and helmets, even with tiger skins around their chests), each of them joining the melody with their bagpipes in full blast, with drums and flutes. They had kept hidden and silent, but they had been standing there from the start: a mighty battalion. I felt as if the little violinist, through his courage, had obtained their intervention out of the darkness. After the final crescendo, the crowd was shouting for joy, and I with them!

But I could absolutely *not* applaud nowadays like I did then. I feel so weak. So, no Edinburgh Festival this year, sadly.

The Swine Flu has by no means turned into a plague; on the contrary, it seems well contained. Communion on the hand is more contagious, some epidemiologists assure, than on the tongue. And yet, after eight weeks the Holy Communion restrictions are still not lifted. His Lordship didn't grant us dispensation. Sunday after Sunday, as on weekdays, I consume at the altar the large Host and the Precious Blood, knowing that all eyes are staring at me from behind, while I'm forbidden from giving the Saviour to my obedient sheep. It would be easier to bear if we at St John's were not the only ones in the diocese prevented from receiving Our Lord. Perhaps, if a fiercer virus deprived the whole country or the entire world from Holy Communion, people would come to love the Holy Eucharist more deeply. Would they not?

Meanwhile, on 7th July last at the Cathedral, Fr Munro offered the EF Mass and gave Holy Communion on the tongue without being reprimanded, Miss McDiarmid told me. Even in the Ordinary Form, I heard, priests have given on the tongue. In our deanery, the Ukrainians receive in the mouth without hindrances. Nowhere in other dioceses has Communion on the tongue been forbidden either. Actually, even in Kinlochlour, Communion on the hand was only "recommended", not commanded. This imposition on God, on the people and on me weighs me down terribly, despite the fair weather. Thankfully Adam asked Fr Munro if he would consider covering for me at

St John's, and he generously drove all the way from Kinlochlour
the last two Sundays. All made a Spiritual Communion, I was
told, as they wouldn't receive on the hand.

Last night we looked at the sky, Jacques, young Henri and I.
Not a single cloud. Stars shone so bright and so numerous! The
right half of the moon was clearly visible. Henri is rather imaginative. A dedicated altar server, he must have been impressed
by our conversation at supper on the Eucharistic embargo. The
missing half of the moon, he fancied, was broken into so many
scattered lights, the stars, "like fragments detached from a Host."
The boy had a point. And yet, I commented, even the brightest
stars are mere matter, while the smallest particle of Host is God.
The suns are His. The crumbs are Him. Like in the Book of the
Apocalypse, when "*The dragon with his tail drew the third part
of the stars of heaven, and cast them to the earth.*" It seems to me
that the "fallen stars" are the Eucharistic fragments sown upon
our altars, falling off the palms of communicants, spread upon
church railings, stuck on hymnbook covers, stamped along
door handles, trampled underfoot, swept away as dust or wax,
ignored; forgotten. Practically denied. For years, for decades,
it didn't seem to bother me. I knew the faith of the Church
about consecrated Hosts, but I was emotionally blind as to
its implications. I didn't choose to end up where I am now. If
anything, this Swine Flu crisis opened my eyes. No longer can
I give the Lord on the hand. I'm sorry.

No longer either can I deprive my people from the Eucharist
while consuming it alone. As long as Holy Mass is allowed, so
should Holy Communion. I'm supposed to go back today and
offer Sunday Mass at St John's, but my heart aches.

MONDAY 28TH SEPTEMBER 2009, KINLOCHLOUR HOSPITAL.
FEAST OF ST WENCESLAS.

If they find me strong enough, tomorrow they will add a
bypass to my cowardly heart. I didn't wish it but my cardiologist

decided that the operation shouldn't be delayed further. I collapsed this morning, on my own at the altar. Thankfully the Sacrifice was completed since I had just swallowed the Precious Blood, even though the Mass wasn't ended. Vera found me unconscious and called the ambulance. My hip is broken, an X-ray confirmed. It wasn't as bad last Thursday: then I didn't faint. I'd only needed to sit down at the Offertory and was able slowly to resume. It's my fault apparently. Last February I was warned to take it easy and to avoid stress. I'm sorry that I failed, again.

I was almost shocked to see His Lordship enter my hospital room an hour ago. Mgr Doogan had told him about my collapse and forthcoming operation. I'm really touched that he popped in literally minutes before departing to England. Mgr Doogan had anointed me last week. His Lordship heard my confession and asked if I was at all able to hear his. Miss McDiarmid came back to my bed after he'd left. She'd been as surprised as I to see His Lordship. I asked her to dispose of my belongings, including my little journal, if ever I didn't wake up tomorrow. She's the one writing down today's entry on her small notebook as my diary remained at the flat. I can't feel most of my body and can barely dictate the words. I'm pleased that my left thumb and forefinger still join at my command. What more do I need to hold the Host and utter "*Domine non sum dignus*"? No last will, since as a religious I possess nothing. Apart from . . . Ah, yes, when I'm gone, the "Saigon *missile*" must be given to my altar server, young Henri Billard. I have an inkling that he might make good use of it.

[*The following is written later in the evening, as dear Father fell asleep during my rosary. On waking up he insisted on dictating further. Is it wise, though?*]

Tomorrow will be St Michael's feast: not a bad day to fly home, if God wills. Home . . . I do believe I'm in the peace of God, although I don't really feel it. We tried everything. Mrs

Heggins sent to her cousin at the Vatican a chronicle of our
Eucharistic crisis. Hoping to ingratiate him, she mentioned what
good friends Elvis and I were! The Monsignor clearly has a soft
spot for poodles, for he told her over the phone that we had
all acted according to the general law of the Church and that
we should not fear. An official letter will be sent from Rome,
he confided. (A similar response to another parish in America
is already online, Adam noticed.)

And yet, when in desperation Mrs Docherty rang Bishop
Wallace this morning to plead the cause of her daughter, he
replied that much to his regret the Swine Flu was still too much
of a threat for the restrictions to be lifted, according to Government experts. She begged him, saying that her seven-year-old
had only received Jesus four times in her life, since the restrictions had begun a month after her First Holy Communion. For
nearly three months now, young Katherine has been denied the
Lord at Mass, when her friends in town receive the Host in the
hand every Sunday. He encouraged her to hope and pray for a
return to normal at Inveroven before Christmas, or to receive
on the hand in Glenangus.

On a couple of occasions the thought occurred to me that,
perhaps, we were being stubborn, inflicting upon ourselves
unnecessary sufferings. Would not future generations despise
us for making a fuss and posing as Eucharistic martyrs? [*Miss
McDiarmid is shaking her head in denegation.*] I dismissed these
ideas. God knows our motives and our hearts. We all offer
up this unfair deprivation. Deep inside, we believe that our
sacrifice is acceptable to God and will bear fruit. [*Miss McDiarmid is nodding at this — and would prefer not to be mentioned here.*] But for how long will this go on, sweet Lord?
Some families drive one hour to Inveroven rather than attend
a non-authorised traditional Mass in Kinlochlour. Their loyalty
is manifest. It breaks my heart not to be able to feed your sheep,
Lord, your little ones.

I don't recall why this virus is called "Swine" flu, but it just struck me that swine are fond of "dung." That's where they live. No wonder this came to me, then. My hope, Lord, is in your "Little Flower." His Lordship has some devotion to her, he once told the priests. Presently, he's leading the diocesan pilgrimage to Lancaster Cathedral where the relics of St Thérèse of Lisieux are on display overnight. I asked Thérèse to take care of this, since I'd failed. She liked my patron saint. So, she'll hear me. She wrote something like: "I have read the lives of many missionaries. The life of Théophane Vénard interested me and touched me more than I can say, because his life was quite ordinary." I think she added, "My soul is like his. He is the one who has best lived my way of spiritual childhood."

I wish I also had. But even though I've failed, Thérèse is hard to disappoint.

[*Following his request, these four smaller pages in my handwriting were inserted at the end of Fr Théophane Dung's journal by me, Bridget McDiarmid (Miss).*]

ATT: THE RT REV FERGUS DOOGAN, BISHOP OF KINLOCHLOUR ON THURSDAY 25TH MARCH 2023

Dear Bishop Fergus,

Further to my letter posted yesterday, it appeared to me on second reading that the Dung Diary *is more relevant to the cause of your late predecessor than I first assumed. While there is little of interest in poor Fr Dung's story, it indirectly illustrates the prompt obedience which characterised Bishop Lennox. I recalled last night that he had found the letter from the Congregation for Divine Worship (a copy is annexed to this letter) on his return from his Lancaster pilgrimage, the day Fr Dung passed away. The letter stressed that Communion on the tongue could not be forbidden, being a universal law of the Latin Church. The very same day he emailed his episcopal council — as we both remember — to inform us that he was immediately lifting the Eucharistic restrictions, since "they had not proved really advantageous."*

I took the liberty of sending a copy of Fr Dung's diary to Fr Adam Brown, MSJS, your successor as Parish Priest of Glenangus. I expect that he will share it with his young assistant Deacon Billard, perhaps as an ordination present next 29th June. (By the way, your red gloves and buskins have arrived on time for our practice.) God works in mysterious ways indeed.

Ewan Munro

X

A Leper on the Swiss Riviera

(2010, SWITZERLAND)

ET AT THE TOP OF A BROWN FRANCISCAN habit, the back of a shaven skull crowned with a ring of shining black hair could be seen above the table, in a gap between two wheel-chairs. "This must be *Fr* Antoine," Ueli von Schtreuli surmised, glancing at the diminutive silhouette from behind. The faceless friar was kneeling upright, his sandals emerging from his cowl spread on the dusty ground. All around, half a dozen *guests*, as they were called, were eating their lunch assisted by volunteers standing at their sides. Fr Antoine was the only one on his knees, probably to make conversation easier with his seated *guests*.

The *guests* were handicapped young people invited and cared for by the High Bailiwick of St Andrew of Cyprus for one week every summer in various European countries: this time in Switzerland. They enjoyed the annual event immensely for the lively entertainment provided and the genuine friendships which developed with the young volunteers of the Bailiwick from one year to the next. The *guests* were made to feel as if their physical or mental handicaps, often very severe ones, had ceased to be obstacles. The young volunteers were lay people, but Catholic chaplains attended as well, enhancing the event with a welcome spiritual dimension.

Swiss Federal Councillor Ueli von Schtreuli kept at some distance from the table while chatting with senior Bailiwick staff. For a man holding such a stressful political office in Bern, spending a few days of vacation by Lake Geneva as a mere member of this Catholic charity was particularly refreshing. He slowly walked around the table and stood on the opposite side, eager to see at last the face of the young friar. His wife had

warned him: "Antoine's new Franciscan colleagues eat upon the
floor, didn't you hear, darling Lili? With no table or chairs, but
only with a skull in the middle of the room. Even worse, no
conversation is allowed during table reading — or 'floor' reading! It's all quite exciting, but why must they say always that
old *Latin* Eucharist — they're so young? Anyhow Lili, I know
exactly what you'll think when you see young Antoine now as
a Franciscan priest: 'What a waste!' you'll grumble. But please
don't make *any* comment. It's good enough that he's come back
to the Bailiwick after six years. And in fairness, our Chantal
never said what she might have felt towards him in the past.
Still, when I think he could have called me 'Mother,' and instead
I now call him 'Father.'"

   "Julienne is often right," Ueli smiled interiorly, as Antoine's
face entered his range of vision. "Clearly, what a *waste!*"

   There had been high hopes that Antoine De Veuster would
join the Bailiwick in some capacity or another. Mothers had
praised him as the ideal son-in-law; fathers had pointed at him
with confidence as a future asset for the Bailiwick's charitable
operations in Lebanon; youngsters liked his fair-play at tennis
and his winning humour; chaplains expected him to rise with
merit to a senior ecclesiastical position. Why had Antoine let
everybody down?

   Ueli remembered the comical or pathetic shift of narratives,
once the hopes of many had been bitterly shattered. Women:
"Say what you want Alice, his hair is too *dark*, and he *smiles*
too much. I don't mind half-Belgian grandchildren (it's easier
than half-French in some respect), but I want them *fair*-haired."
Men: "Arabic at Louvain, why not? But to get a *1st* was a mistake: it puts off head hunters because they think the boy too
academic for collaborative work. Believe me, a 2.1 is what he
should have aimed for, like I did — or even a mere 2.2 like you,
Gaston." Girls: "I can't believe he *won't* dance anymore except
with animals, as he claims St Francis did. Imagine that, Antoine

hugging birds, or goats: Fie!" Young men: "You're mistaken. My cousin was his classmate at *Les Chamois*. They were fourteen years of age and he doesn't recall Antoine getting up on one ski on his very *first* waterski attempt on the lake. Perhaps on his second or third attempt, though. Not that it matters much now, of course." Priests: "Why wouldn't he become a nuncio like his uncle, Mgr d'Aviernoz? Why join this so-called *Traditional Seraphic Family* instead, a tiny, radical and precarious gathering of originals, when so many solid mainstream institutions would have welcomed him with arms wide open!"

Lunch was over and now the culprit stood, broad-shouldered and thinly bearded, of high stature in his Franciscan robe, with his gaze disconcertingly clear. Would not some slight flaw show, to make wasting a man like Antoine easier to admit? Ueli felt wanting in his presence, both in size and in grace. But unlike his fellow-participants in the summer camp, Federal Councillor von Schtreuli didn't mind. As a politician he was used to gauging others (and to being judged by them), so that he felt enriched rather than belittled by outstanding human specimens. He'd met many exceptional persons, admittedly, and lost some, like his dear friend Heinz Müller, a recently deceased cabinet maker or rather, as Ueli claimed, an unassuming genius! "We're both 'cabinet' men," was their private joke when queried about their unexpected friendship.

Fr Antoine was now pushing the wheel-chair of his *guest* towards the kiosk where, half an hour later, a jazz performance would take place. Ueli was glad that the dates he'd suggested for this 2010 edition of the Bailiwick European Summer Camp overlapped with the Montreux International Jazz Festival. He admired the magnificent view across Lake Geneva with the Alps in the background. It looked nearly as attractive, admittedly, as Lake Zurich where he'd spent his childhood. A saxophone could be heard in the distance. Had Fr Antoine any notion, Ueli smiled, of who Miles Davis was?

The Eucharistic celebration took place the following morning in the sport hall of Saint-Beix, the village where the Bailiwick was holding its camp. Two volunteers walked behind and next to each *guest* in a wheelchair or on crutches. The High Bailiff had come in person from Nicosia, while the Archbishop Protector would only arrive from Rome three days later. The knights and dames in full liturgical gowns processed towards the platform set against the back wall. Stepping ceremoniously upon the coloured basketball and volleyball lines decorating the smooth floor *did* feel slightly awkward, Ueli thought. With the International Olympic Committee Headquarters visible in the distance on the Lausanne bank of the Lake, one could have been forgiven for confusing the liturgical event with a parade for the Paralympics. He was almost surprised to find that Antoine was taking part, standing behind a wheelchair. The last one in the procession as chief celebrant, Mgr Paul Eigerhoff finally ascended the podium. Walking to the opposite side of the makeshift altar, he then faced the congregation who, after a brief moment of stupefaction, burst into laughter.

Mgr Eigerhoff's voice was audible enough through his plastic mask representing German Chancellor Angela Merkel: "Friends, this *is* me, and yet this *is* not me. For too long we have worn masks, haven't we? We hid from people. We put on a show. No more, though. In this 2010 European Summer Camp of the Bailiwick, we're going to learn to appear for what we are. We're going to take off our masks." Which he did, eloquently tearing poor plastic Angela Merkel in halves (with some difficulty). His round brown face now visible, he went on: "The High Bailiwick of St Andrew of Cyprus has a long tradition of assistance to those in need. But unlike certain military orders, *we* never shed blood to fulfil our mission, whether in the Crusades or later. We are gathered here to care for our *guests*. But *they* also take care of us. Dear less-abled friends, you teach us that handicaps by no means suffice to define a man or a woman. You make us think and look into ourselves, and we discover that we're all hindered, deep inside, by pride, fear, and pretence in many ways. But this week, we'll learn to accept who we are and who others are."

In the afternoon, after a substantial lunch on the terrace of his hotel facing the Lake, Ueli von Schtreuli woke up from his siesta with his mind made up. He *would* accept prefacing the special edition of Krueller's catalogue. The famous Bernese auctioneer was organising a historic sale of all the furniture inventoried in Heinz Müller's workshop and domicile. Paradoxically, almost no one had ever heard the name of the genius cabinet maker. Krueller Auctioneers hoped that a preface by Federal Councillor Ueli von Schtreuli would pique the curiosity of its clientele far outside the federal capital and even abroad. As to Ueli, he was quite pleased to honour his friend's memory (in addition, displaying his expertise in local craftsmanship was politically advantageous). By now he had put together enough material, he reckoned, for a pleasant tribute to the deceased.

He missed Heinz. Their friendship had started unexpectedly in 1998 at a party in Gstaad, given by Lord Yehudi Menuhin, a *musical* genius. It was Ueli's very first term as Federal Councillor. He congratulated the old violinist on the exquisite restoration of an authentic Mathäus Funk chest of drawers. The ageing maestro had smiled mischievously and, introducing his cook Wanda, had confided that she bore full responsibility for the improvement. Not that *she* had restored the precious piece of furniture: instead, she had put her employer in contact with Heinz Müller, her devoted husband. Back in Bern, Ueli had strolled toward Müller's workshop, nearly missing the entrance. In a modest residential area, along a quiet street, no sign indicated the presence of such a craftsman. In a backyard, the magical "workshop" looked more like a rural timber storage space. Expressing no noticeable awe on this his first encounter with a Federal Councillor, Heinz's round figure welcomed the visitor with a smiling face. He looked like a hearty baker in a Christmas tale. Comically, the very first thing he asked Ueli was whether he could press his fingers inside the drawer of a Louis XV *deux-corps* to keep the freshly glued protection paper in position until it dried. Ueli had felt at home in that room as, perhaps, never before.

*   *   *

The following morning, Abbé Vignettaz was looking with interest into the bottom of his nearly empty coffee cup. He was not attempting to read the future in coffee grounds, though. Rather, the priest was merely trying to hide his embarrassment. As the Chaplain of the *Suisse Romande* Chapter of the Baili-wick, Abbé Vignettaz was in charge of the liturgy for this 2010 edition of the Camp. It was in that capacity, he explained to Ueli, that he had invited Fr Antoine De Veuster to take part. Of course, before accepting, Antoine had been congenially upfront about his offering the traditional Franciscan rite exclusively. Abbé Vignettaz had assured that he would secure an altar for Antoine's daily private Mass.

"So, why did M. le Curé of Saint-Beix deny Fr Antoine access to his church, since he'd given you his permission three months ago?" the Federal Councillor enquired, having already guessed the motive.

Abbé Vignettaz pretended to sip a remnant of coffee from his empty cup before answering:

"Well, yesterday afternoon M. le Curé Jean-Pierre Ursy asked me why Antoine didn't offer his Mass with the other priests in the sport hall. I said that he doesn't concelebrate. M. le Curé Ursy then suggested that Fr Antoine scheduled his Mass alone in the sport hall later on. I informed Fr Antoine who responded that he'd rather not, as people come and go in there outside of the Camp Mass, and also because it is not a sacred place, as he had expected. So, I went to M. le Curé Ursy again this morning. He was upset to hear Antoine's answer, and even more when

I had to tell him that Antoine uses only the traditional Latin missal. That was the end of it, sadly, as he was going to be late for performing in Montreux."

"How do you mean? Is the Curé a jazz musician?"

"Apparently he plays the saxophone."

"I see. And where would Fr Antoine offer his Mass today, then?"

"I don't know. Between us, I think he might consider leaving the camp discreetly, were it not for the *guests* (they like him to bits). He's wondering whether it's dignified enough for him to preside over the Eucharist in his bedroom, at 'Chalet Paradis' where the clergy are staying. The slight problem is that his room is located under the roof with little headroom for lifting his arms at the Elevation of the Host, I fear. Also, from tomorrow he will have to share the bedroom with the Dominican chaplain from Turin, whose arrival at the Camp was delayed. We're lucky that Fr Antoine had brought his vestments and chalice with him. I gave him a bottle of Fendant wine. I'm afraid it's the best I could do."

"Perhaps, but your best is still much less than what you had promised Fr Antoine. This reflects rather poorly on the hospitality of the Bailiwick." With a stern face, Ueli von Schtreuli walked the sheepish Abbé Vignettaz to the door. Interiorly though, he was toying with the idea of becoming involved in that petty disagreement. He quite liked Fr Antoine, and the Religious Affairs Department was part of his portfolio. Solving this minor difficulty could be a pleasant summer recreation compared with the conundrum of the Bishop of Zagh, he fancied. It had taken him nearly a year to have that ultra-conservative prelate "promoted" to a position of Observer at the United Nations in Geneva, after his cathedral canons had started rebelling against their bishop, who was radically hostile to lay ministers of the Sacrament of Anointing, among other things. In fairness, Ueli didn't consider himself a progressive. Turned a Catholic twenty-eight years earlier when courting the pretty Julienne Brignoz-Fressen, and after reception by then-*Fr* Paul Eigerhoff, a leading ecumenist, at heart Ueli had remained loyal to his Zwinglian ancestors on doctrines such as the sacredness of the State, although unlike Zwingli he preferred democracy to aristocracy. Despite Fr Eigerhoff's recommendation "not to overdo it" as a new Catholic, he also held slightly broader views than Zwingli about the Eucharistic Bread, especially when the State religion supported it. Such was the case in Fribourg, where his brother-in-law and the heads of the other patrician families, members of the cantonal Senate, walked in tailcoat before the Blessed Sacrament, each holding in his white-gloved hand a medieval lantern with his family coat of arms. As to the diocese of Zagh, well, the Government needed peace in the Canton for the sake of the forthcoming tax reform (the French and the Germans were relentlessly pressuring Switzerland to tackle "tax evasion" on their behalf). So, peace he had secured. In addition to the rank of archbishop for the demoted prelate of Zagh, his Geneva assignment included a monthly trip to New York, compassionately flying First Class.

*   *   *

One hour before supper, a raspy tone could be heard, or a smoky vibration felt, rather, through the front door of Saint-Beix Presbytery. His finger on the doorbell button, Ueli stood still, impressed by the talent of M. le Curé Jean-Pierre Ursy as a saxophonist. Yes, no wonder this man was allowed to perform at the Montreux Festival! Ueli von Schtreuli had received an email forwarded by his Department that afternoon. It was from Fr Ursy who had heard of his presence at Saint-Beix and was "requesting a visit if his valuable time allowed, for advice about a fellow priest causing him perplexity." Ueli had been happily surprised that the local Curé would take the initiative of a discussion about the request of poor Fr Antoine for a church altar. Hence his standing confidently outside the Presbytery. Having pressed the doorbell button, Ueli was let in by the priest. The puzzled visitor could still hear a sax playing, obviously not by his host. After a saxophonist handshake (pressing one knuckle and gripping three fingers only?), Fr Ursy showed him the CD he was listening to. Ueli was glad to have refreshed his jazz classics as it made the encounter more auspicious. They sat down and started chatting. Fr Ursy seemed to know his whiskeys no less than his jazz: the Dalmore was worth its reputation.

"I don't expect you to recall our earlier and brief encounter, Councillor, since you meet with so many people. It was at the Geneva Opera House for *The Magic Flute* performance, organised by the Swiss Rotary Club in support of overpopulation containment in Bangladesh."

"Ah? Yes, indeed. Was it about four years ago, or three? Much as I like Mozart, I found the production a bit conventional, if I recall correctly. Why must Tamino *always* wear leather, and why must Papageno *always* look like a half plucked chicken? Is it all in the libretto? On the contrary, having the Queen of the Night carried on what looked like a *sedia gestatoria*, with ostrich feather fans, was original, albeit a bit pointed. However, I hear that your interest lies with jazz, rather than opera."

"I'm not a professional saxophonist, surely not, Councillor. But the Festival attracts nearly 250,000 spectators every year on my doorstep. I had to do something about it. It's my third year as a free-stage performer, with friends. For the occasion I wear a Roman collar: they dubbed me 'Padre Saxo.' Councillor, I believe very deeply that music can bring peace to the world."

"Father Jean-Pierre, how insightful of you. You know what, Lord Yehudi Menuhin — the legendary violinist — told me about the same thing once, at his residence in Gstaad. We need more men of culture and diversity like him — and you. Although not a Christian, Lord Menuhin appreciated ritual worship for its cultural value, even in the Christian religion, I remember. For instance, he'd signed that petition to Pope Paul VI in support of the traditional Roman rite. Alas, such open-mindedness is to be found only in exceptional men."

"I share your concern, Councillor. Even among us priests, you know, this is a rare quality. Take a local case like this unfortunate Fr Dieudonné Diouff. He's been parochial administrator *ad interim* in Montreux for ten months only, and already intransigence is rife among Catholics down there, so I hear. No wonder: because his father is from Senegal, he thinks he can get away with neo-colonialist homilies. You won't believe it, but he openly stated that 'his race was deeply indebted' to the French missionaries who brought Catholicism to his country. Not a word about the brutal eradication of tribal customs and the looting of mineral and agricultural resources; not to mention slavery! He even boasted of having been baptised by Archbishop Marcel Lefebvre in Dakar. Between us, I have it as a fact that Diouff had lunch at the headquarters of those integrists: at Ecône, further up the Rhône. Meanwhile, he has no time for jazz whatsoever. No time for jazz... Simply ludicrous. Imagine a parish priest at Bayreuth having no time for Wagner! Thankfully, a former Eucharistic minister of Diouff assured me that if a broad-minded priest succeeded him in Montreux, peace (and religion) would flourish again, so she said."

A veteran politician, Ueli understood exactly where his musical interlocutor was leading him. Decoding innuendos was the more pleasant aspect of his profession, actually. Clearly then, Fr Ursy had *not* invited him to discuss Fr Antoine's private Mass, but rather to seek his own promotion to the fashionable parish of Montreux. Ueli felt a bit vexed at the misunderstanding. On the other hand, he was honoured by the tacit acknowledgement of his influence in these matters—greater indeed than a Catholic bishop's. But he wasn't sure whether he was ready to collaborate. In truth, he was a bit somnolent—perhaps that late-afternoon whiskey?—and didn't feel in the mood for business while comfortably sitting in such a deep leather armchair, with an elegant copy of Bruegel's *Tower of Babel* in its silver and ebony frame on the left wall. The occasion was for relaxation, as further dictated by the splendid view over Lake Geneva in front of them, mirroring the dazzling sun, high in the cloudless July sky. Ueli thus selected from his facial vocabulary a professionall y-concerned-yet-noncommittal frowning of eyebrows and tightening of lips. His silence could be read as approval, inviting Fr Ursy to document the scandal further if conceivable; but it also allowed him to keep his opinion to himself and his cards very close to his chest. For good measure, as if adding punctuation to his non-verbal phrase, he rested his hands upside down upon his knees, palms exposed in dignified helplessness, as a clear indication that assistance *was* to be sought indeed, plausibly from heaven, if not from him.

Realising after a silence that Councillor von Schtreuli was not as yet offering his mediation, Fr Ursy stood up to push aside a vase on the credence table near Ueli: "Sorry, these acacia branches are in your face. There, that's better." Reaching his desk, he then warned: "About Fr Diouff, sadly there's worse, Councillor, much worse. As the Swiss citizen with chief responsibility over matters of religion, no doubt you'd wish to act against such an attack on civic harmony perpetrated by a Catholic priest. In my hand is Fr Diouff's parish newsletter from last Lent, four months before the beginning of the Montreux Festival, if you permit me to read it for you. Here it goes . . . ."

"Dear parishioners, I was born in West Africa. Therefore, allow me to speak about the origins of jazz music. I regret that my people invented it. France colonised West Africa from the seventeenth century onwards. Among other tribes, many Dahomeans ended up as slaves in Louisiana. I quote from a reliable source that: 'Dahomeans who worshipped vodun *(spirit) and the snake god,* Damballa, *brought rituals to New Orleans that became known as voodoo — elements of which appeared in early blues and jazz. Various bluesmen referenced* mojo hands *and* black cats, *and*

*jazz pioneer Jelly Roll Morton blamed a voodoo curse for ill
health and a declining career.' Friends, while we welcome into
our town every visitor of good will, we as Catholics must also
beware of evil influence, often at work unbeknownst to us. A
major contribution by the French missionaries in Senegal, my
home country, was to cast out evil spirits and to break curses,
as Jesus commanded his apostles to do after his example. We
miss this year in the Lectionary the parable of the* Return of
the Unclean Spirit. *I invite you to read it in your bible in St
Matthew's and St Luke's Gospels. Brethren, let us keep watch, lest
the evil one regain control and make our new condition worse
than before he had been expelled. Let us ask the Holy Mother
to touch the hearts and to bring to Jesus all the performers, staff
and visitors for the forthcoming Jazz Festival in our town. These
good people are our brothers and sisters, just fond of a particular
style of music. We love music as well. Let us check only which
tune we dance to. How beautiful the music of conversion, the
music of mercy, the music of truth and of salvation."*

"And how untimely this quote," Ueli moaned interiorly... He
vaguely remembered a note sent to his Department that past
spring about, "bigoted opposition to the Swiss Riviera's major
cultural and touristic event." He had decided to let it sleep at
the time, being too busy with more important issues (such as
the Bishop of Zagh's "promotion"). Now he was annoyed to
have been dragged back into business when, after all, he was
on holiday. He thanked Fr Ursy for his sense of civic duty,
agreeing that something had to be done: "If this matter were
only about worship, creed, or morality, investigation would
pertain to your bishop. But since you fear for public order and
the economy, you did well to let me know. I will call Fr Diouff
today." However, to prevent the priest from thinking himself
the outright winner in their little battle of wits, he added: "At
least, I'm pleased to have heard that Fr Diouff doesn't deny the
historical fact of slavery, to his credit."

*   *   *

While brushing his teeth that evening, Ueli thought that he'd done well not to plead for Fr Antoine's need of an altar at Saint-Beix Church. Earlier at the Presbytery M. le Curé Jean-Pierre Ursy had given him the solution without a fight, perhaps unwittingly. Ueli had rung Fr Dieudonné Diouff at Montreux. He hadn't said a word about the Jazz Festival or the Lenten parish bulletin. He'd only mentioned the need for a wall-facing altar for an Old Rite private Mass. And sure enough, a side chapel at Sacré-Cœur Church awaited Fr Antoine for his traditional Franciscan Mass every day of the Camp. At least that job was done, with nobody hurt.

"Enough worries for the day." Sitting at the desk in the lounge of their suite while Julienne was getting ready for the night in the adjacent bedroom, Ueli opened with relish the draft of his Preface for the Krueller's Auction House catalogue. "I owe dear Heinz an hour of my time. Here we are..."

Heinz Müller and the Spirit of Restoration, a Preface by Federal Councillor Ueli von Schtreuli.

Very few in Bern, in Switzerland and even fewer abroad, know what loss the world of arts and crafts suffered with the death of cabinet maker Heinz Müller last 19 April (2010). And yet, experts praised him as second only to our glorious Bernese Mathäus Funk (1697–1783). As a long time friend of the deceased, I am honoured by the request of Krueller's Auction House to write this Preface to their autumn catalogue for the sale of the Heinz and Wanda Müller Collection.

Heinz held the view that antiques and historical interiors often had a turbulent history: these events left their mark. To remove them would be to rob the object of its past, of its identity. A great deal of original substance, especially from the surfaces of antique furniture, has been lost or destroyed. It is therefore all the more important ...

"Ueli? Are you not coming to bed? Your camomile is getting cold, you know? Also, I have something to tell you, Lili."

"Yes darling, I'm nearly there."

It is therefore all the more important to secure and preserve the existing stock, old surfaces and the patina. This preservation and restoration includes: cleaning, retouching and refreshing old surfaces, re-gluing all loosened veneer parts, strengthening loosened structural connections, adding missing veneers and restoring functionality, replacing any drawer guides that have leaked out, repositioning the jammed doors, repairing the locks and, if required by aesthetics, also replacing parts damaged by insect attack. The task of the restorer is to preserve old surfaces and the patina, but at the same time to restore the functionality of an object. For instance, Heinz once boldly widened the inner compartment in the replica of a Louis XVI secretary to fit exactly sheets of paper of the modern A4 size. Similarly, he dared to drill an access into the rear of another piece for the wire of a small printer concealed in an antique desk replica.

"Lili, the clip on my necklace is jammed. Can you open it for me, please?"

"Sure, here I am. Yes, you're right, it *is* stuck. I don't want to break it. There you are. But, you never take off your pearls before going to bed normally, do you? Anyway, I only need another few minutes. I'll drink the camomile as it is. Fine."

Heinz Müller had no known religious affiliation. One day, feeling so happy at the beauty of creation and not knowing whom to thank for it, he opened his window and shouted: 'Thank you.' Heinz was curious and without bias. One Shrove Tuesday I told him that I couldn't come to the workshop the following day because I would go straight from the office to church, it being Ash Wednesday. Heinz was touched by the symbolism of the ashes as a reminder of human mortality. As a lover of wood, he wrote this short meditation.

'Ecce Lignum — Behold the wood: The wood is a work of art in itself. I try to make its given structures clearer and, with little mechanical effort, to guide the viewer's attention to further discover and to be astonished by the versatility of creation. Whoever has eyes to see, let them see! What the wood contains, raw or worked upon, brings about new life. Nature is the creator and artist; I am

only a tool and a midwife, to recover the treasure and make it accessible to others.'

"Lili, darling? So, you don't want to know my little achievement of this afternoon? Yawwwwwn... I'm really exhausted now, after pushing the wheelchair of my *guest* uphill all the way to the archery ground. Thankfully Fr Antoine helped me and my *guest* went to confession to him. I thought *I* might do the same. Would *you*? By the way, I'm glad someone is working out a solution for his Mass. Night night then."

"Yes darling, yes, yes. It's good news, but I really *must* finish this work. Good night."

Modern flatpack furniture was totally alien to Heinz. A trip to IKEA would have been his most accurate conception of Purgatory. Furniture made of compressed sawdust or woodchips was to him what cement would have been to a sculptor like Michelangelo. He would not have denied the practical usefulness of these processed materials. But he would have been acutely aware of their lack of soul. Heinz cared about inner growth. He praised the nature of wood — and of the many varieties of woods — as innate principles of growth developing from within, by contrast with conditioning artificially applied from without. Heinz insisted that no classical piece of furniture can be restored or created on an assembly line, the way cars or laptops are produced. Each piece is unique, like a child.

"Very well, Mr Federal Councillor, your wife won't tell you what she did this afternoon after pushing the wheel-chair of her *guest*. Or I'll just whisper it, to see if you're actually listening. There: I rang Fr Antoine's ..."

Heinz told me he was not an inventor. Rather he was all about restoring the substance of the object impaired by aging, damage and interventions, with the greatest possible preservation of that traditional substance. All along though, he believed that characteristic traces providing information about age and use (that is, the history of the object) should be carefully considered.

Heinz Müller became the anonymous revivalist and disciple of our great Bernese ébéniste Mathäus Funk (1697–1783). But Funk would have conveniently subcontracted to fellow craftsmen the work which did not involve wood only. Because the know-how was sadly lost, Heinz Müller had to learn all by himself the multiple skills needed to restore such works of art as classical pieces of furniture, in addition to those of cabinet maker. For instance, inlay consists of cutting out a solid body of one material to receive sections of another to form the surface pattern. Marquetry applies pieces of veneer to a structure to form decorative patterns, designs or pictures. To cover the inside of the furniture, paste paper manufacturing requires colouring by hand traditional paper (known as 'Herrnhuter Kleisterpapier') with a brush and spreading it evenly with as little glue as possible. Heinz did all this by himself. What about the marble tops covering many Funk pieces? Heinz managed to buy the very last (colossal) block of marble from the original Bernese quarry used by Funk two centuries earlier, checking that it didn't conceal a significant hollow or inner bubble, as sometimes occurs. Heinz sliced and carved the marble tops himself. Lastly, he manufactured according to traditional techniques all metal components such as locks, keys and hinges.

"I've finished reading my magazine, Lili. Are you *still* working? In case you can't find it in the dark, darling, I left your djellaba folded on *your* side of the bed. I'm using mine as a nightgown. Will you do the same?"

"Sure. I'm coming."

"Good. It's much more comfortable than pyjamas, and your brother will be pleased to know that we made use of the gifts he brought us back from Cairo. Unless you change your mind of course, and wear yours as Lawrence of Arabia for the Camp's fancy dress party tomorrow, and I can be Nefertiti. Now I'm falling asleep. Shake me gently if I snore."

In our modern era of specialisation, who could combine such a range of artistic skills and use them to such a degree of competence?

Readers will forgive me for suggesting that only names such as those of Michelangelo, Raphael or Leonardo match this criterion. Were they not architects, painters, sculptors and poets all at once? Obviously far remote from the glories of the Italian Renaissance, whether in time, place or fame, dear Heinz was just an anonymous Bernese craftsman. But what an example of professional dedication and integrity he gave us! No one acquainted with his legacy can ever again look at classical furniture with indifference, or handle these pieces as mere commodities or financial investments. Something of their maker's soul still speaks to us through them. Master Müller, we salute you; dear Heinz, we thank you; and we hope that some readers will hear the call to further and expand the revival you single-handedly started.

Ueli was quite pleased with his Preface. Although brief, it was detailed enough and not too technical. Only when getting into bed did he realise what Julienne had mentioned about Fr Antoine. "Working on a solution for Antoine's Masses?" How could *she* know about his phone call to Fr Diouff before supper? Sitting at table opposite Nicolas Michel, the former Head of Legal at the United Nations, he'd only found five seconds to reassure Fr Antoine that, "A solution had been found for his Mass." Had M. le Curé Jean-Pierre Ursy then spoken with Julienne about Montreux? But he didn't know about Ueli's successful petition to Fr Diouff for Fr Antoine's private Mass. Fr Jean-Pierre Ursy was a very able man, surely. Ueli dismissed the suspicion that M. le Curé of Saint-Beix had perhaps denied an altar to Fr Antoine merely to secure a private meeting with the Federal Councillor and express his suitability for the advantageous parish of Montreux. Such an assumption felt unfairly tortuous.

Julienne was fast asleep. Ueli looked at his wife, her silhouette barely discernible in the dark bedroom. He felt guilty for having let her down that evening. Once again. She'd wished to be with him and he'd ignored it, preferring to write his Preface. But she'd mentioned that *djellaba* again, hadn't she? Really, how infuriating she could be at times. No, he would *not* be seen or photographed as "Lawrence of Arabia"—especially not one month after the constitutional ban on minarets all across the country—with two hundred Bailiwick *guests* and staff smiling! He found "his" folded djellaba and was about to hide it in his suitcase. Was she wearing hers? Little Julienne... He suddenly felt a surge of tenderness for her. Despite her lack of concern for political issues, or merely for discussing topics dear to his heart such as Heinz Müller's achievements, she had proved a crucial support not only in his career, but primarily as his wife. No one knew him, understood him better than she. And there she was, asleep like a little girl with her fancy dress on, his forty-eight-year-old better part and the mother of their Chantal... He couldn't do, he realised, without her whimsical intuitions, her colourful levity and her warm steadfastness. She was his treasure.

All this, it struck him, Fr Antoine would never know. The joy of giving life, of holding in his arms the fruit of shared loved as he'd held their new-born Chantal some twenty-five years earlier, Antoine would never experience either. And yet, the young Franciscan seemed normal and even fulfilled. No, much more than that, Ueli reckoned in all honesty, and perplexity. As if unaware of the great expectations set on him of old (not least by mothers and daughters, Ueli remembered) and now forever thwarted, Fr Antoine De Veuster looked superlatively sane and contagiously happy. *What* kept that young man going? He didn't play the saxophone. What drove him? What was *his* secret? He wore a robe, if not a djellaba. He wasn't Aladdin or Lawrence of Arabia and yet he claimed—or had?—special powers and gambled his entire life on one idea which he called a Person; on one word which had to be whispered in Latin and concealed from hearing and sight, as if the world's salvation depended on it. Did it?

Ueli tightened his eye mask, expecting to dream of classical furniture.

*   *   *

It was the Federal Councillor's habit to jog for a full twenty minutes first thing in the morning, followed by his bodyguard. But the path through the steep vineyards covering the Swiss Riviera on the north-east banks of Lake Geneva had proved tough to run on an empty stomach. As Ueli had been slowing down, the sound of incoming email on his mobile phone had offered him an honourable reason to pause and check the latest message.

"Dear Councillor von Schtreuli,

"Greetings and thank you for your visit yesterday afternoon. I am sorry to email you early this morning, forwarding to you below an electronic message received during the night from the Vatican. I cannot hide from you that I am hurt by it. Our friendly conversation and your appreciation of the need for clerical change in Montreux had let me hope for a broad-minded solution. Instead, I realise that pressure was put on the Holy See to intervene in a very secondary issue. I will of course provide an altar at Saint-Beix for Fr Antoine De Veuster. I can't see that there was need to bother the Vatican with what must look like a trifle to them.

"As you could see yesterday from my interest in modern music, I am not an antiquarian. Under obedience, then, will I have such a medieval form of the Eucharist celebrated in my church. Forgive me if I don't wish Fr De Veuster success in restoring his out-of-date worship for the few elitist Christians possibly interested. As to me, I hope to serve the cause of peace through active involvement with the quarter of a million visitors at the Montreux Jazz Festival. Should you wish to support this ministry of mine as protectively as Fr De Veuster's, you will find me and my 69,044 Twitter followers ever grateful. *So mote it be.*

"Respectfully yours,

"Padre Saxo

"FW: To the diligent attention of Rev Fr Jean-Pierre Ursy, Parish
  Priest, Saint-Beix, Switzerland
"Prot.: 07/2010
"URGENT
"ATT: Rev Fr Jean-Pierre Ursy, Parish Priest, Saint-Beix Presbytery,
  Saint-Beix, Canton de Vaud, Confédération Helvétique—by
  email
"From the Vatican, Tuesday 13th July 2010

"Dear Fr Ursy,
  "This dicastery has recently been informed that a priest from
the *Traditional Seraphic Family*, Fr Antoine De Veuster, was
faced with difficulties for offering his private Masses according
to the Extraordinary Form of the Roman rite in a place of
worship within your parish.
  "Allow me to support heartily the request, respectful and
legitimate, made by this priest. It would not be understandable,
especially one month after the happy conclusion of the *Year for
Priests*, and in the spirit of reconciliation wished by the Holy
Father as expressed in the Motu Proprio *Summorum Pontificum*,
that a priest member of an institute of pontifical right be prevented from honouring the promises of his ordination through
celebrating the sacred mysteries of the Mass, as entrusted to
him by the Church.
  "Trusting in your understanding and your diligence in
answering favourably this legitimate request, I assure you, dear
Father, of my heartfelt and friendly consideration, with my best
wishes for your own ministry.
  "D. Gregorio di Pippo, SdB, Archbishop Secretary"

The Federal Counsellor was standing amidst the steep vine-
yard, wiping the sweat off his face while reading the message on
his phone. Still panting at first, then perplexed, and finally blushing again—although not out of physical exhaustion—Ueli had

read with deep frustration Fr Ursy's early communication. Who could have interfered with his plan, and behind his back? Fr Antoine himself? Surely not, Ueli reckoned — not quite his style. That inept Abbé Vignettaz? Too incompetent, it seemed. Mgr Paul Eigerhoff? He wouldn't move a finger to facilitate a Latin Mass. Whoever the culprit was, no wonder Fr Ursy was furious and suspected him of double-dealing. Ueli quickly looked up the Twitter page of "Padre Saxo." Yes, quite a following! And what was worse, the "Jazz priest" had the explicit support of the *Riviera Lodge of Worshipful Friends of Orient*, well-known for their love of saxophone apparently, among other interests . . .

Surely, "Padre Saxo" was a man with many musical friends. Should he, a Federal Councillor, expect them to play some scratchy tune against him, electorally speaking? That was Ueli's real concern. Yet another problem he would have liked to be spared. What bother! The only thing to do was to have his secretary in Bern buy a (second-hand) saxophone as an emergency and meet him down by the Lake in Montreux later that day with some television crew. He hadn't the slightest clue how to play the damn instrument, but the potential damage would be sufficiently contained, for now, by a news item showing Federal Councillor Ueli von Schtreuli playing the sax at the Montreux International Jazz Festival. Next, and easier to manage, Ueli had to cancel the booking with Fr Diouff for Fr Antoine's Masses at Sacré-Cœur Church in Montreux, since the Vatican's injunction for the Mass to take place at Saint-Beix took precedence. What a mess! And what a waste of his time, when he could have been polishing his Preface to Heinz Müller's catalogue! It wasn't the holiday he'd expected.

*   *   *

Back at the chalet, Ueli hadn't needed to question Julienne during her breakfast.

"Good morning darling! Why, you're red like a goldfish! Did

you just run all the way down the mountain? But wait, before you shower, I must tell you something funny."

"I simply can't, Julienne. Bad emails just received, which I must see to immediately."

"A pity, Fr Antoine has ..."

"What? What with Fr Antoine? Please, out with it. It's important!"

"Don't shout! What's the matter with you? I thought you had urgent business to deal with?" Holding her glass of orange juice as if for a toast, Julienne had announced: "Fine. You can congratulate me on my diplomatic prowess, darling Councillor. Fr Antoine can now say Mass here at Saint-Beix. I meant to tell you yesterday night but you were too busy writing. (I thought we'd agreed on *no* work after supper this week?) Anyhow, yesterday afternoon I asked Fr Antoine why he was hearing confessions during our Eucharistic Celebration instead of concelebrating with the other chaplains."

"That was Abbé Vignettaz's job to deal with, Julienne, not yours!"

"Sorry, I was just being charitable to poor Antoine. So, he explained his reasons. I didn't get it all but I was *shocked* to hear that he had no church for his Mass in the Franciscan rite. Would you believe that his new roommate from Turin even threatened to leave the Camp if he said a Latin Eucharist in their bedroom? That old Italian affirmed that he 'wouldn't let a baby priest have it his way,' when older generations had had to put up with the *aggiornamento* at great personal and pastoral cost' — or something like that. He soon apologised: no one can be angry at Antoine for long."

"What? Julienne, I need to tell you that ... Really I'm quite ...."

"What again, Mister Grumpy? I know, I know. You think the Latin thing is extreme and should not be supported by mainstream personalities. (There, have a glass of orange juice. That will do you good.) And I haven't forgotten that 'my actions as your wife can alter the way you're perceived as a public figure.' But what was I to do darling? I simply *love* St Francis! He spoke to birds and even to wolves, you know? But he wouldn't ring the Nuncio his uncle for a solution — *Antoine* wouldn't, I mean, not St Francis. (By the way, did *you* know Mgr d'Aviernoz is being sent back to Europe? That's promising for his nephew's career. Don't worry: I didn't say *that* to the bishop.) So, on my insisting, Antoine allowed me to do so if I wished, being part of the staff at this Camp."

"No! Julienne, don't tell me that *you* rang . . . ."

"Wait, I haven't finished. So, the Nuncio didn't sound too encouraging over the phone, but he was friendly to *me*. He even enquired about your health issue last year. I reminded him that it wasn't your kidney, but your *bladder*. In passing, he warned us that a sudden loss of weight could be an alarming symptom. *I'm* surely healthy then, I replied. (I hope I wasn't being too familiar with His Excellency; but we're about the same age, so it doesn't really matter, does it?)"

"Fantastic! I'm deeply relieved that the Pope's ambassador is monitoring my bowels, thanks to my wife. I hope it will be on the front cover of *L'Osservatore Romano*."

"Stop being naughty, Lili! If you interrupt me continuously, I will never be ready on time with all the *guests* by the bus car park in — heavens! — in *eight* minutes . . . It's today we visit St Maurice Abbey, and Antoine will preach on the Martyrs of the Theban Legion, and Fr Ursy has offered to play the saxophone at the Offertory: we're all thrilled! I must leave you at once! But, briefly then, while you were out running, Fr Antoine popped in to thank me. He was all smile and tan, still with his medieval tonsure, when — (you know, this vocation of his really *is* a waste for the Bailiwick, and Bérengère thinks just the same, and so does Chantal, but we agreed that it can't be helped now, so, better support him — at least that's what we thought as women; that is, as mums and daughter). And... Where was I? Yes, when Fr Antoine announced that the parish priest's secretary next door had just rang 'Chalet Paradis.' And what was she ringing about, you wonder?"

"What was she ringing about, your husband wonders..."

"Don't tease me. Well, she was asking about his preferred time for saying his Eucharist at Saint-Beix Church privately. Isn't it marvellous? He won't need to say it at his *Chalet Paradis* now. (Antoine is a witty Franciscan, you know. He said it made sense, as 'there would be no Mass in paradise ever' — he meant, 'in heaven.') The Nuncio must have rung the parish this morning and told them Antoine was okay. But *we* all knew that from the start, didn't we? So, all is well that ends well. You see, I leave the Religious Affairs to you, darling Councillor, but next time you hear of a quick fix needed for simple problems, Lili, why don't you just ask a housewife?"

ABOUT THE AUTHOR

Born in 1971 in the Loire Valley, Fr Armand de Malleray, FSSP left France in 1994 after completing a Master's Degree in Literature at the Sorbonne in Paris. He taught French at the Military Academy in Budapest before joining the Priestly Fraternity of St Peter in 1995 in Bavaria, where he was ordained in 2001. His first priestly assignment was in London, Southwark Archdiocese. He served in England since, apart from five years in Switzerland, then in an administrative position at his Fraternity's headquarters. Since 2008, he has been the editor of *Dowry*, the quarterly magazine of his Fraternity in the UK & Ireland. Fr de Malleray has been chaplain to the international *Juventutem* youth movement since its inception in 2004 (cf. www.juventutem.org), and to the Confraternity of St Peter, his Fraternity's international prayer-network for priestly vocations. Since 2015, he is the rector of St Mary's Shrine in Warrington, Liverpool Archdiocese, where he also oversees the apostolate of his Fraternity in England and promotes vocations to the priesthood and to the religious life.

WORKS BY THE SAME AUTHOR:

X-Ray of the Priest in a Field Hospital
Essay (Waterloo, ON: Arouca Press, 2020)

Ego Eimi: It is I — Falling in Eucharistic Love
Essay (Ireland: Lumen Fidei, 2018)

Italian Renaissance, Art for Souls
Art commentary
CD-Rom (Versailles, France: Rejoyce, 2004)

Caravage, l'art pour l'âme
Art commentary
CD-Rom (Versailles, France: Rejoyce, 2001)

La Tour, l'art pour l'âme
Art commentary
CD-Rom (Versailles, France: Rejoyce, 2000)